"Fake News" Theology

How and Why We Use Biblical Authority to Dodge God's Authority

The 2020 Lenten Lectures of the
Episcopal Diocese of Philadelphia (PA)

Kenton L. Sparks

CASCADE *Books* · Eugene, Oregon

"FAKE NEWS" THEOLOGY
How and Why We Use Biblical Authority to Dodge God's Authority

Cascade Books
An Imprint of Wipf and Stock Publishers
199 W. 8th Ave., Suite 3
Eugene, OR 97401

www.wipfandstock.com

PAPERBACK ISBN: 978-1-7252-7032-9
HARDCOVER ISBN: 978-1-7252-7033-6
EBOOK ISBN: 978-1-7252-7034-3

Cataloguing-in-Publication data:

Names: Sparks, Kenton L., author.

Title: "Fake news" theology : how and why we use biblical authority to dodge God's authority / by Kenton L. Sparks.

Description: Eugene, OR: Cascade Books, 2020. | Includes bibliographical references.

Identifiers: ISBN 978-1-7252-7032-9 (paperback). | ISBN 978-1-7252-7033-6 (hardcover). | ISBN 978-1-7252-7034-3 (ebook).

Subjects: LCSH: Bible—Criticism, interpretation, etc. | Bible—Hermeneutics. | Bible—Theology.

Classification: BS476 s681 2020 (print). | BS476 (epub).

Manufactured in the U.S.A.   03/26/20

For those who wish to love God and neighbor,
including their enemies

Contents

Acknowledgments

This text is an expanded version of the Lenten Lectures of the Episcopal Diocese of Philadelphia (PA), delivered on March 7, 2020. Those who attended can essentially review the lectures by reading the text, but with the added benefit of the supporting documentation, relevant bibliographic sources, and more detailed explanations of the various issues and their possible solutions. The possible benefit for those who did not attend the lectures is obvious, though it remains for them to judge whether this benefit is worth the investment of their time. At least the book is not very long. I have retained in this printed version the language of "lecture" but with certain adjustments for a written form, the most obvious being that I assume an audience of readers rather than listeners.

The title of the lectures, "Fake News Theology," is apropos to my present social context in the United States at a critical juncture in our theological and political history. While I do not know what the shelf-life might be on a "popular" title like this, I'm quite sure the issues tackled in the lectures are neither new nor apt to expire any time soon. The Church has a long history of naively believing and committing itself to false- or half-truths, sometimes because of innocent mistakes but in other cases, unfortunately, as acts of willful ignorance. The results of these errors are not inconsequential. The original lectures were, and the published version is, a modest attempt to provide theological resources for the Church as we confront this threat to the gospel.

I am very grateful to Reverend Richard Morgan, Rector of the Church of the Good Samaritan (Paoli, PA), for the invitation to present these lectures, and to the Episcopal Diocese of Philadelphia for supporting them.

The manuscript for this book was prepared in only a few weeks from the first typed word to publication. For this I must thank my incredible and capable Executive Assistant, Kim Lownes, and the editorial team at Cascade Books (Wipf and Stock Publishers), who moved the manuscript from submission to publication in only two weeks. Any errors of form or substance are, however, my own.

Kenton L. Sparks

Provost, Eastern University

Season of Lent, 2020

Abbreviations

AB	Anchor Bible
ACCS	Ancient Christian Commentary on Scripture
BJS	Brown Judaic Studies
CBQ	*Catholic Biblical Quarterly*
CTJ	*Calvin Theological Journal*
JETS	*Journal of the Evangelical Theological Society*
KJV	King James Version
LCL	Loeb Classical Library
LXX	Septuagint
NCamBC	New Cambridge Bible Commentary
NCBC	New Century Bible Commentary
NICNT	New International Commentary on the New Testament
NIV	New International Version
NRSV	New Revised Standard Version
OTL	Old Testament Library
RHR	*Revue de l'histoire des religions*
RSV	Revised Standard Version
SBT	Studies in Biblical Theology
SJT	*Scottish Journal of Theology*
ThTo	*Theology Today*
VT	*Vetus Testamentum*
WTJ	*Westminster Theological Journal*

Introduction

O ur country is deeply divided these days. On one side are those who understand and believe "the facts," and on the other are those who gullibly embrace the phony "alternative facts." It is obvious, however, that "the truth" in this debate lies in the eye of the beholder. No matter what side we stand on, all of us believe that *our side* stands for the facts and that the other side doesn't. *We* understand; *they* are clueless.

I'm quite sure that this open conflict, often dubbed the "culture war," will not be resolved today. Perhaps it should not be resolved but must be won by one side or the other, or by some still-to-emerge perspective that's better than either (or any) of the current alternatives. But in spite of our profound divisions, I suspect that we can begin our discussion on a point of profound agreement. Namely, I suspect that all of us believe a lot of people have been fooled by fake news, and that this phony news has been and shall continue to be damaging and dangerous for our society. For we have seen, perhaps more clearly than ever before, that millions of people can be fooled into receiving what is false as what is true, and that this exchange of the truth for a lie can and will have serious consequences for us, our world, and generations to follow.

My primary theme today is certainly not political, though it may have some bearing on how we think about and evaluate political questions. Rather, my task is to draw out and examine what I believe is a very common but mistaken pattern within Christian theology. Namely, I believe that Christians often construct systems of biblical authority that paradoxically allow us to circumvent and evade the authority of God in the Church and in our personal lives. I will suggest that these approaches to the Bible, in which we essentially end up quoting the Bible against God, are based on "fake news" about what the Bible is and how it should be read. This "fake news" theology opens up Christians to manipulations and errors because it subtly allows us to more easily replace the voice of God with our own fallen, human voices.

I should say that this error, if I have understood it correctly, is by no means the only or worst kind of theological blunder that Christians can make. There are as many ways to err in our theological and ethical judgments as there are human beings. But this "fake news" phenomenon, and its connection with biblical authority, seems uniquely problematic in our current social and ecclesial context.

Lest I be misunderstood at the outset, I should stake out several of the fundamental theological assumptions for this discussion. I will assume, in keeping with Church dogma, that God exists, that God has dramatically addressed the human condition through the person of Jesus Christ, and that the Bible serves, in one way or another, as the written and authoritative word of God. I will also assume that humanity suffers under broken conditions, in which we commit sins of commission and omission, known and unknown, and that all of us stand in need of essential spiritual healing, not to mention psychological, social, and physical healing. Within this general and orthodox context, my goal is not to question the authoritative role of Scripture in our theology but rather to question certain approaches to biblical authority that may not suit either the nature of Scripture itself or the ultimate authority of God in our theology.

Some readers perhaps struggle with or question some of these basic dogmatic claims. I have a deep sense of respect for these doubts but cannot address them directly within the scope of these lectures, though I will touch along the way on themes that have implications for our understanding of doubt in relation to, and in the context of, theological dogma.

The Apostle Paul counseled his church at Thessalonika "to consider everything but hold fast to what is good" (1 Thess 5:21).[1] It was—and still is—excellent advice.

---

1. A paraphrase of the NRSV: "but test everything; hold fast to what is good."

——— *Lecture One* ———

In the Beginning Was the Truth

"If you continue in my word, you are truly my disciples; and you will know the truth, and the truth will make you free."

—JOHN 8:31–32

M ost readers will be familiar with the first verse of the Bible: "In the beginning, God created the heavens and the earth" (Gen 1:1). There follows a brief but detailed description of how God properly ordered the cosmos, from the stars in the sky to living things, culminating finally in the creation of humanity. Within a few chapters this order is disrupted by humanity, first by transgressing the order of creation (Gen 3) and then, more violently, by resorting to murder (Gen 4). The narrative thus sets the stage for a certain kind of theology, which sees the creation as a broken but still orderly pattern. As I said, all of this is likely familiar to you. Less familiar may be that this creation theme is explicitly developed in two other parts of the Bible, one in the Old Testament and the other in the New Testament.

Creation and Truth in the Wisdom Literature

First, we find in the wisdom tradition of the Old Testament that "wisdom" (*ḥokmāh*) is presented as God's co-worker in the creation process (Murphy 1990:118–21, 133–49).[1] This is especially striking in Proverbs chapter 8, where wisdom, personified as a woman, stands beside Yahweh as a "master worker" (*'āmôn*) as he creates the land, skies, waters and humanity.[2] That this was God's procedure in creation was considered important by Israel's sages, for it implied that they could discern from a study of the created order the divine wisdom behind it (O'Dowd 2007). The sages observed nature and human behavior, identified the underlying patterns, and distilled the truths they learned in poetic essays, admonitions, pithy maxims, and mind-bending riddles. One could summarize their viewpoint with the famous dictum of Socrates, that "the unexamined life is not worth living,"[3] but one of the sages expressed this less elegantly when he compared the unexamined life to that of a "brute beast" (Ps 73:22).[4]

The sages were certainly interested in practical wisdom but sought, when possible, to infer from it still deeper truths about God and things divine. One of these fundamental theological truths was the law of retribution, by which God blessed righteous people and cursed the doers of evil. Proverbs is replete with admonitions to this effect, that the good will live long in success and the bad will die young and in squalor. Some of the sages further explored and raised serious questions about this tit-for-tat theology, especially in the wisdom books of Job and Qohelet (i.e., Ecclesiastes),[5] but retributive theology remained an enduring theme in the wisdom tradition and Jewish theology. Centuries later, during the time of Jesus, some of the rabbis still believed that catastrophes and

1. For an introduction to the Hebrew wisdom tradition, see Murphy 1994.

2. The Hebrew term *'āmôn* is probably a loanword from the Akkadian wisdom tradition, where the *ummānu* was a divine or semi-divine figure that brought culture and skill to humanity. See Clifford 1999:100–101.

3. From Plato's "Apology," see Fowler 1942:133.

4. Ps 73 is a wisdom poem that addresses the perennial theme of the "prosperous villain" (Crenshaw 1980:183).

5. Questions about retributive theology are also implied in some of the Proverbs, such as this one: "Better to be poor and walk in integrity than to be crooked in one's ways even though rich" (28:6).

physical ailments were evidence of God's judgment against sin (cf. John 9:2–3; Luke 13:4).

The sages learned from experience that one must *choose* to pursue wisdom, so they devoted considerable space in Proverbs (see chapters 1–9) to the task of recruiting the reader into their quest for truth. Their prospective students were primarily young men, as we'd expect given the patriarchal society of ancient Israel. The choice was presented as a proverbial fork in the road of life, in which one path, that of wisdom (*ḥokmāh*), leads to success and long life, and the other, of folly (*'iwwelet*), leads to failure and death. Certain Hebrew terms and concepts are commonly attached to each of these paths.

Related to the first path are words like knowledge (*da'at*), understanding (*bîn*), truth (*'emet*), discretion (*mezimmāh*), justice (*mišpāṭ*), righteousness (*ṣedeq*), and goodness (*ṭôv*), which together denote and are related to the achievements of wisdom. Also connected with this path are words like teaching (*leqaḥ, tôrāh*), counsel (*'ēṣāh*), correction (*mûsār*), and reproof (*tôkaḥat*), which convey the fundamental importance of what we would call the virtues of learning.[6] Anyone on the path of truth must be inquisitive, observant, and teachable; they must be able to change viewpoints and positions as new evidence and arguments are considered. As the sages expressed it, "Whoever heeds instruction is on the path to life, but one who rejects a rebuke goes astray" (Prov 10:17). In sum, the wisdom tradition assumes that we cannot grow wise unless we're ready to recognize and address our errors, weaknesses, and failures.

The path of wisdom required a good bit of what we would call "book learning," to such an extent that one of the sages warned his readers to avoid too much reading (Qoh 12:12). Most of these books were apparently lost long ago. Oral traditions were even more important, as is implied by the oral character of proverbial wisdom and the repeated admonitions in Proverbs that students

---

6. For an accessible introduction to what is known as "virtue epistemology," see Wood 1998. For a more robust discussion, see Roberts and Wood 2007.

should listen to the instructions of their mothers and fathers, as well as of their teachers (Prov 1:8; 6:20; 23:22).

The sages studied and taught about themes that in our own day would fall under categories like emotional and social intelligence, communication and leadership strategy, peace and friendship theory, social ethics, morality, the art of persuasion, and the virtues of industry and hard work. But if one wished to follow this better path successfully, they agreed that the most important qualification was to harbor in one's heart a deep "fear of Yahweh" (*yir'at yhwh*). Permutations of the phrase, "the fear of Yahweh is the beginning of wisdom," appear five times in the wisdom corpus, more than any other line of biblical wisdom (see Prov 1:7; 9:10; 15:33; Ps 111:10; Job 28:28). Theologians have sometimes attempted to define this fear in terms of "respect" or "commitment" rather than violence, as if God is too patient and loving to be an actual object of fear, but the wisdom books were written within a tradition that knows little of this line of thought. According to the sages, Yahweh stood ready to curse in anger those who did not walk the path of truth (Prov 3:33; 15:25; 29:22) and to discipline with love any soul who strayed from it (Prov 3:11–12; 15:10). But of this the sages were fully confident: for those who fear God and follow the path of wisdom, the results are far more valuable than piles of silver and gold (Prov 3:14; 8:10; 8:19; 16:16).

The crooked path that leads to destruction is described with a different set of terms. Here another female is set before the would-be sage, this time known as "folly" (*'wwelet*). By choosing between the two women, wisdom and folly, young men set their courses for life (O'Dowd 2007:72). Those who choose folly are suitably called "fools" (*'ĕwîl*), but we're given a richer picture of these lost souls by two other titles given to them, that they are "simple" (*petî*) and are "scoffers" (*lēṣ*). When Proverbs describes the fool as "simple," it portrays him as immature, unformed, and naive (Whybray 1994:33; cf. McKane 1970:273). He tends to believe whatever is said in his circle of friends (Prov 14:15) and, having chosen the path of folly, finds himself guided only by the insight of "ne'er do wells" (Prov 13:20; 14:7). If he had selected a different path with different friends, perhaps things would have turned out better. When the English translations describe the fool as a "scoffer" or (in some versions) as a "mocker," these are our best guesses for the meaning of the underlying Hebrew term *lēṣ* (Richardson 1955). While the meaning is not entirely clear, we can infer from biblical uses of the word that the *lēṣ* took an active role in challenging truth and goodness, in some cases by concocting his own "false news" versions of wisdom (Prov 14:6). He is described in Prov 21:25 as "proud" (*zēd*) and "haughty" (*yāhîr*) and "arrogant" (*zādôn*) because he has closed himself off, mainly for personal and selfish reasons, from the traditions of knowledge found on the path of true wisdom. The fundamental contrast between the scoffer and the wise is described well in the advice of Prov 9:8: "If you rebuke a scoffer, he will hate you; but if you rebuke a wise man, he will love you."[7]

As we have noted, the sages who penned the book of Proverbs were committed to the path of wisdom and truth but also to the "fear of Yahweh." They were thus confronted by an important question, namely, whether they could and should profit from the wisdom of foreign sages who did not know the God of Israel and in fact were probably devoted to some other deity or deities. In the end, they took the less insular path and decided that all truth is God's truth, no matter who recognizes it. This is especially evident in Prov 22–23, which contains material adapted from an Egyptian text, the Wisdom of Amenemope (see Sparks 2005:70–71; Fox 2009:705–33), and in Prov 31, which includes a contribution from the non-Israelite mother of Lemuel, King of Massa (Fox 2009:882–85); the same may be true of sayings of Agur, in Proverbs 30. The sages were apparently well-versed in foreign literature and it is very likely that other parts of Proverbs were taken from (or influenced by) this foreign corpus even where it is not evident. Their commitment to an all-out search for the truth, wherever it could be found, will provide an important touchpoint for our discussion. A key difference between the sage and the fool was that the sage was open to the outside world of learning whereas the fool

---

7. Paraphrased by the author for style.

was more insular, and depended on information provided by his narrow circle of misguided friends.

In sum, the sages have laid out for us two possible options for conducting our lives, one that follows the path of wisdom and searches for the truth wherever it may be found, and another that is content to accept false views of God and the human condition.

Creation and Truth in the Gospel of John

Now as I said, the creation story of Genesis is developed in two key parts of the Bible, not only in the Old Testament, as we have just seen, but also in the New Testament. The gospel of John is introduced with this memorable if convoluted paragraph:

> In the beginning was the Word, and the Word was with God, and the Word was God. He was in the beginning with God. All things came into being through him, and without him not one thing came into being. What has come into being in him was life, and the life was the light of all people. The light shines in the darkness, and the darkness did not overcome it. (John 1:1–5)[8]

The allusion to Gen 1 is very clear. Just as Proverbs connects the biblical creation with wisdom, knowledge, and truth, so John connects the creative word of God in Genesis with the incarnate "word" of God, Jesus the messiah. He is the "light" that brings truth into the darkness: "Whoever lives by the truth comes into the light, so that it may be seen plainly that what they have done has been done in the sight of God" (John 3:21). The concepts of "word" and "light" and "truth" are fundamental in John's theology, for these are the sources that can reconnect our broken situation to the world of goodness and order.

John uses the Greek term *logos* ("word") more often—and with more metaphorical power—than any other biblical author. As he uses it, the *logos* refers not merely to written and spoken words from

8. All quotations are from the New Revised Standard Version (NRSV) unless otherwise noted.

God but more significantly to Jesus himself as the truest and fullest "word" from God. In fact, to see Jesus is, in John's theology, nothing other than to see God the Father himself (John 14:9). This is why Jesus is "the light that enlightens every person" (John 1:9).

The Greek word *phōs*, meaning "light," occurs twenty-three times in the gospel of John. Again, this is more than in any other biblical source. The same can be said of its antonym, *skotia*, which means "darkness" and occurs fourteen times. That these words are spiritual metaphors for our status in relation to God, whether for or against him (or perhaps, whether we are lost or found), can stand without detailed comment. By contrasting spiritual light with darkness, John has laid out his own version of the two paths we saw in the Old Testament wisdom texts. The wise person of Proverbs is the one who in John walks in the light, and the fool in Proverbs is the one who walks in darkness. More specifically, John identifies those who walk in the light as persons who are attracted to and embrace God's revelation in Jesus the messiah. I should point out, however, that John's portrait of the created order is less optimistic than we find in Proverbs. Proverbs generally assumes an order with disordered exceptions, whereas John's world is much darker and more broken. Jesus is the "light of the world" because the whole world lives in sin and darkness (John 8:12).

John's concern for the lost and darkened creation and for the importance of applying "truth" to its condition is evident in his vocabulary. He uses the word *kosmos* ("world") fifty-seven times, which is far more than any other New Testament author, and the same can be said about the word *alētheia* ("truth"), which he uses twenty-five times.[9] My point here is not to fully explore how John understands and develops these concepts but rather to show how his gospel is focalized on guiding the reader from the path of darkness into the light of the truth.

To summarize: Proverbs and John interpret God's creative activity as providing not only the necessary conditions for human life but also the foundation for what is good and right and true. In a world gone astray, this true foundation, to which the world

9. Spicq 1994:1.76–81 (*alētheia*).

should return, is depicted in Proverbs as the path of wisdom and in John as walking in the light. These healthy paths are contrasted in the sources with the dark path of folly, falsehood, and evil, which leads to death. In other words, not only is it true that "In the beginning, God created the heavens and the earth," but also that "In the beginning was the truth."

The Priority of "Truth" in Scripture

My objective so far has been to remind us of something I believe many in the Church have lost, namely that the Bible itself calls us not only to defend but also to seek and embrace "the truth." Now Christians have a long history of defending what they believe to be true. We've fought "culture wars" and even literal wars over matters of doctrinal purity and religious freedom (Nolan 2006). But we have seen in our brief review of the creation tradition, as developed in the Old and New Testaments, that God's people are more properly ordered when we not only defend but habitually seek out the truth. For it is implied in Proverbs and John that, when we are fools walking in darkness, we do not realize that we've actually taken the wrong path rather than the best path. When this is our situation, we may actually end up defending what is false as if it were true. That this is a real threat can be readily illustrated by two biblical examples, one each from the Old and New Testaments.

Truth in the Story of Job

The Old Testament contains many memorable stories, among them the somewhat disturbing story of Job.[10] I will assume that

10. The book of Job was not written all at once but rather by a series of editors with somewhat different theological perspectives. I am partial to Snaith's account of the book's origins (1968), but no single model of Job's composition can be proved correct. Because it is my practice to give voice to all of these editors, the composition history of the book is not directly relevant to my discussion.

readers are generally familiar with this story but for the sake of clarity will briefly review it.

Job is a righteous man who suddenly faces trouble, including the deaths of his children and a very serious illness. The reader is provided with an explanation for this, to the effect that God is allowing his chief adversary (śāṭān) to test and prove the authenticity of Job's deep faith.[11] We must note, as readers, that none of the characters in the story—not Job, not his wife, and not his friends—are provided with this explanation. They must figure out for themselves why a man with Job's spiritual pedigree is suffering as he is.

Job's friends accuse him of committing some kind of egregious sin. They do not know what this sin was, but they are quite confident, based on the intensity of the punishment, that Job's suffering can only be caused by God's curse, and that God's curse can only arise when sins have been committed. Job insists in response that his walk is blameless and that he is innocent (Job 9:15; 34:5), but his friends counter with equal confidence that this is nonsense because everyone sins, and the fixed pattern of life is that "those who plow iniquity and sow trouble reap the same" (4:8, 17–19). In fact, one of his friends made the bold claim that no innocent person had *ever* perished (4:7).

If we evaluate the story of Job in terms of the two paths laid out in Proverbs, the paths of wisdom and folly, we quickly see that this story develops entirely within the first path. Job is a man of wisdom, but so are his friends. There are no fools in the room. We see this last point plainly in the encouragements the friends give to Job, which will strike us as very orthodox and wise:

> How happy is the one whom God reproves; therefore do
> not despise the discipline of the Almighty. (Job 5:17)

> If you will seek God
> and make supplication to the Almighty,

11. The Hebrew word śāṭān has the definite article and should be read in English as "the satan" or, better, "the adversary." The word is not functioning for the author of Job as a proper noun meaning "Satan."

> if you are pure and upright,
> > surely then he will rouse himself for you
> > and restore to you your rightful place.
> Though your beginning was small,
> > your latter days will be very great. (Job 8:5–7)

These are principles commonly espoused by the sages in the book of Proverbs, as is the more general assumption behind them that God punishes evil and rewards what is good. It must have frustrated some or many of the ancient sages when they read the conclusion of the story. Rather than agree with Job's "orthodox" critics, God declared that Job was right and his friends were wrong: "My wrath is kindled against you . . . for you have not spoken of me what is right, as my servant Job has" (Job 42:7). Notable here is that God does not merely take a side; he is angry with Job's friends, to such an extent that his wrath can be assuaged only if they offer sacrifices and if Job prays for them (Job 42:8).

How and why did Job's friends err? Basically, they applied their principles of wisdom too rigidly to a complex world. While reality certainly has its patterns and we do well to recognize and apply them to life, in the end, the human condition does not fit neatly into our tidy categories; still less can God be crammed into them. Good theology thus requires more nuance than Job's friends gave to it, and that is where they went wrong. But we would profit, I think, by asking a somewhat deeper question: Why did Job's friends, and the people they represented, prefer their rigid approach to theology over something more nuanced and true to life? I will address this question later in the lecture.

Meanwhile, there is more to learn about human knowledge and theology from Job. Although God declares in the end that Job has bested his friends in the work of theology, he also levels some harsh criticisms at Job in chapters 38–41:

> Then Yahweh answered Job out of the whirlwind:
> "Who is this that darkens counsel by words without
> > knowledge?
> Gird up your loins like a man,
> > I will question you, and you shall declare to me.

Where were you when I laid the foundation of the earth?
Tell me, if you have understanding . . .

Gird up your loins like a man;
I will question you, and you declare to me.
Will you even put me in the wrong?
Will you condemn me that you may be justified?
Have you an arm like God,
and can you thunder with a voice like his?
(Job 38:1–4; 40:7–9)

Job seems to have deserved this criticism. He openly confronted God at numerous points in the story, more or less accusing God of injustices against him. Job demanded his day in court with a boast that he would "fill [his] mouth with arguments" so that "[God] would listen to him" (23:4, 6). One gets the impression from all of this that Job is innocent only in comparison with his more confused friends, for in the end, even Job himself repents in "dust and ashes" (Job 42:1–6). Job is confused; but his friends are much more confused.

We should note with care that the concerns addressed by the author of Job were not merely theological, in an intellectual sense, but also profoundly spiritual, moral, and ethical. When we read the book with a bit of empathy, we can sense how painful it must have been for the ancients to suffer profoundly and receive in the process a steady stream of judgments and insults from their religious friends. Job addresses this directly at points, especially in Job chapter 6:

Those who withhold kindness from a friend
forsake the fear of the Almighty.
My companions are treacherous like a torrent-bed,
like freshets that pass away,
that run dark with ice,
turbid with melting snow.
In time of heat they disappear;
when it is hot, they vanish from their place. (Job 6:14–17)

We can add to this a long list of texts in which Job complains that his friends have turned against him . . . that they mock, and scorn, and abhor him like some misfit (Job 6:27; 12:4; 16:20; 19:14, 19). Though he begs for their pity (Job 19:21), they turn against him all the more as the dialogue unfolds. Literally, they added insult to injury with each line of their "advice." The chief error of Job's friends was not in their view of guilt and suffering, although they were indeed wrong about that. Rather, their chief error was that their love of doctrine and purity seems to have trumped their love for Job. They simply forgot to act as friends and thus became his enemies.

Let us look back now over our discussion of these two wisdom books, Proverbs and Job. If we combine the insights of these books into a hierarchy of insight, ranking those with more knowledge as compared to those with less, we will end up with four levels of understanding. From high to low, the ranking is: (1) God, (2) Job, (3) Job's friends, and (4) the Fools. Those at the bottom of the list, the fools, have no genuine interest in the truth *per se*. Truth is useful to them only insofar as it enables them to do the foolish and hurtful things they do. At the next level, among Job's friends, we find those who seem to care deeply about the truth but are unable to enter fully into the evidence before them. Life is simply more complex than they are able to tolerate. Next comes Job, who is able to ask hard questions about the conventional wisdom because he has experienced first-hand the complexities and ambiguities of the human condition. He is prepared to let reality shape his categories rather than the other way around. He is still a human being, however, and this is why he finally repents in dust and ashes. Though we can say in convenient short-hand that Job was "right" and his friends were "wrong," we would more precisely say that Job and his friends were partly right and partly wrong, but in a way that made Job's partial understanding of human suffering more complete and healthy than that of his friends. For it is only at the top of this hierarchy, with God, that "the truth, the whole truth, and nothing but the truth" finally wins the day. Expressed metaphorically, God sees the "Truth" with a capital "T" whereas our human perspectives yield nothing better than "truth" with a small "t" . . . and all too often "Errors" with a capital "E."

In keeping with what I've just said about life's complexity, I would caution the reader at this point that I've not offered this four-level hierarchy as a fixed point of reference for how things work. It is, as I've said, a heuristic tool, which illustrates how some people can be more serious about the truth than others, and arrive at clearer understandings than others, without conflating the best of human wisdom with God's wisdom. God, and God alone, is the final judge of truth and error. And lest we assume too quickly that we stand on the penultimate level with Job, I'll end this part of our discussion with an appropriate Proverb: "Do you see persons wise in their own eyes? There is more hope for fools than for them" (Prov 26:12).

Truth in the Conflict between Jesus and His Enemies

When we consider the words and deeds of Jesus, as we're about to do, we enter into a minefield where almost every claim we make is strongly contested by one or more very competent scholars.[12] The basic reason for this is easy to see. Scholars have prepared books known as "Gospel Harmonies," which place the four gospels in parallel lines or columns next to each other.[13] When we observe and compare the different versions of the same stories, it becomes clear that the four gospels do not tell precisely the same story about Jesus and sometimes contradict each other. To cite a mundane example, Jesus tells the disciples in Mark's gospel that they *should* carry a walking staff along during their mission work but tells them in Matthew and Luke that they *should not* bring a staff (Matt 10:10). Similarly, we're told in Mark's gospel (15:25) that Jesus was crucified at the *third hour* of the day (i.e., around 9 a.m.) while the time is the *sixth hour* (i.e., around noon) in John's

12. For an accessible introduction to the study of the "historical Jesus," see Beilby and Eddy 2009.

13. My favorite English language harmony is Swanson 1984.

gospel (19:14). The documented list of these discrepancies is very long, and I should add that the differences were in some cases much more than mere slips of the pen. In that last example, most scholars believe that Mark's third hour is correct and that John, which reports the sixth hour, has moved the day and time of the crucifixion so that Jesus died at the same hour as the Jewish Passover lambs (Bonsirven 1952; Brown 1970:882–83). As this and other examples would show, the four evangelists significantly edited their sources and also creatively reshaped the narratives to convey their theological insights. To summarize: the gospel writers do not always and precisely tell us what Jesus actually said and did.

Although I am especially interested theologically in what Jesus himself taught, I agree with Dale Allison's thesis (2009) that the theological perspectives of the four gospel writers, as interpreters of Jesus, are also important and significant for the Christian thought. If we set aside what the gospel writers themselves thought and believed, we could as easily set aside from our theology the writings of Paul and the other biblical authors, not to mention the later insights of people like Augustine, Aquinas, Catherine, Julian, Teresa, Luther, Calvin, and Hooker.

For this reason and others to come, I'll not attend closely in my discussion to the differences between the "Jesus of history" and the "Jesus of faith."

At this point we can pick up my main theme in this section. As is well known, Jesus operated during his brief ministry in an ongoing conflict with certain segments of Jewish society. The traditional list of antagonists included the lay Pharisees and those connected to the priestly classes, not only the priests themselves but also the scribes, teachers of the law, and Sadducees. We should not paint too broadly here with our brush, for Jesus apparently had some friends from these groups (of which Nicodemus the Pharisee is a good example), but on the whole it's clear that the resistance to his ministry came from the religious "movers and shakers" of Jewish society.

One point of conflict between Jesus and these groups centered on their respective approaches to biblical law. A good example is provided in Mark chapter 7, when Jesus and his disciples are criticized by the scribes and Pharisees for eating meals with unwashed hands. This was a clean break with some Jewish legal traditions, which held that ceremonial washing was required before eating a meal. Before we consider the response of Jesus to the Pharisees, we should first consider the source of their Jewish tradition.

No biblical law strictly requires that hands be washed before common meals. But ritual washings are very common within the laws, and we know that in early Judaism some or many Jews extended the application of biblical law to a broader range of situations (Collins 2007:344). This end was often pursued by creating oral laws that stood alongside the written biblical laws and provided guidance for their interpretation (Strack and Stemberger 1992:35–49). One purpose of the oral law was to create a "fence" (sûg: literally, "hedge") around the written law so it would not be transgressed.[14] Eventually these oral traditions were written down in the Mishnah, but this was done several centuries after the time of Jesus.[15] There is a Mishnaic law similar to this one in tractate Ḥagigah 2:5.[16] Jesus seems to have rejected these oral traditions, as did the Sadducees and Samaritans (Bohak 1997:600).

In light of this, we can better understand the response of Jesus. He responded to their criticism with criticism, to the effect that the Pharisees had attached to the law of God an additional handwashing law concocted by human beings: "You abandon the commandment of God and hold to human tradition" (Mark 7:8). If we step back from the situation a bit, we could infer here that Jesus was picking an unnecessary fight over a petty detail. What harm is done, after all, if one is required to wash hands before dinner? Did not our own parents, some twenty centuries later,

14. m. Aboth 1:1; see Danby 1933:446.

15. The Mishnah was codified around 200 CE and provides the basic core of the Talmudic traditions. For an introduction, see Strack and Stemberger 1992:119–66.

16. Danby 1933:213.

require the same thing? But I suspect more was at stake here than it seems at first blush.

Jesus continued his response with a further, critical observation about the law of the Pharisees. Among their laws was the rule of *korban* (Aramaic, *qorbān*), which held that money set aside as a gift for God could no longer be used to assist family members in need, particularly mothers and fathers.[17] Jesus judged that the *korban* rule was constructed in a way, and being applied in a way, that circumvented the requirements of the fifth commandment that children should "honor (and thus care for) their mother and father. He then added: "And you [Pharisees] do many things like this" (Mark 7:13).

We see here that Jesus, as an interpreter of the law, did not criticize the Jewish leaders merely because they were adding new laws to the biblical laws. In another tradition, found in the gospel of Matthew (Matt 23:2–3), he actually acknowledges their authoritative role as teachers of the people. Rather, he confronted the Pharisees and scribes because their oral law fundamentally conflicted with the objective of the written law, which was to ensure that parents were loved and cared for by their children. We can surmise that he rejected Jewish hand-washing rules for the same reason. Purity rules like these perpetuated the boundaries of separation between the elites of Jewish society and the common people, of whom Jesus was one. In essence, these particular Pharisees were interpreting the Bible so that they could dodge God's actual law, which called the Jewish people into a life of love for their parents, the poor, and their neighbors.

And let us remember just now that Jesus eventually became one of their victims. These Jewish leaders, as representative of orthodoxy, were so opposed to the Nazarene that they orchestrated with Rome his execution. We should not reduce their motives to just one thing, but certainly they hated Jesus because they did not like his approach to Scripture.

---

17. For the history and development of this and related votive practices, see Benovitz 1998:1–16.

The author of Mark does not tell us directly what the Phari-sees hoped to gain with their *korban* theology, but we can perhaps infer something of their motive based on insights from other texts and sources. Jesus says in his Sermon on the Mount that these Jewish leaders (not all Jewish leaders!) often paraded their righteous acts before other people, apparently to impress them (Matt 6:1). This would secure certain base pleasures, such as a sense of spiritual superiority and divine approval, as well as their privileged status within Jewish society. Jesus, in his critique of the *korban* law, essentially calls them out for prioritizing these personal benefits (psychological and social) above the more important but less visible priority of caring for parents.

The behavior of the Pharisees in this case illustrates a concept that will be important for our discussion, especially in lecture four. Several decades ago, John Welwood (1984), a psychologist, pointed out that human beings often use religious arguments to support and defend our unhealthy behaviors. He famously described this as "spiritual bypass," in that ostensibly spiritual tools are used, paradoxically, to avoid dealing with our spiritual darkness and blindness. When we prefer "fake news" over truth and facts, this is probably a symptom of this bypass phenomenon.

Summary: The Two Paths

We have seen so far that the Old and New Testaments each lay out a version of the two paths before us, one, based on truth, that leads to wisdom and salvation, and the other, based on falsehood, that leads to error and sin. We noted along the way that those who presume to walk the first path all too often either walk it in error, as Job's friends did, or perhaps have taken entirely to the wrong path without realizing it, as was true of the opponents of Jesus. We also noticed that in both cases these errors were emphatically condemned by God as errors not merely of confusion but of serious sin. Job's friends and the Pharisees were not committed to an all-out pursuit of the truth because they were committed deeply to something false and were unwilling to let it go.

Of particular importance is that in both cases—Job's friends and the Pharisees—the opponents of truth were orthodox people. They were not heretics but rather people of faith committed fully to the basic theological truths of God and Scripture. Job's friends drew their wisdom from the book of Proverbs, and the Pharisees from the law of Moses. I would add that they were also intellectually gifted people. The poetic arguments of Job's friends are elegant and filled with insight, and the oral laws of the Pharisees—as found in the Mishnah—are exceedingly detailed and complex. How and why, then, did these intelligent, orthodox people err as they did? This is the key question for us to consider during these lectures.

I am sure that you have realized at this point, if not from the discussion from the lecture title, that I will suggest in these lectures that the Church has often fallen into the same error as Job's friends and the Pharisees. I offer this as a possibility for you to consider. And if we are to explore this issue without falling into the very same trap, we must commit ourselves, and if necessary recommit ourselves, to a journey that seeks out the truth, including even the inconvenient truths that will upset our sense of the theological and social order. "In the beginning God created the heavens and the earth" . . . and "In the beginning was wisdom" . . . and "In the beginning was the word" and, as I have argued, "In the beginning was the truth."

While God is the creator of truth, it turns out that we can only return to God in a healthy way if we commit ourselves to the path of truth that leads back to God. A spiritual journey without the truth will not bring us closer to God or each other but rather will result in the kinds of conflict and pain we see between Job and his friends. It is not a pretty sight.

What Is the Bible?
The Foundational Approach

*"Now faith will totter if the authority of Scripture begins to
shake. And then, if faith totters, love itself will grow cold."*

—St. Augustine[1]

We have seen that the friends of Job and the Pharisees were
orthodox people, committed deeply to Scripture and to the
application of Scripture to our human context. We have seen, too,
that they erred in this endeavor, in that they applied Scripture in a
way that harmed Job in the first case and Jewish parents in the second. We will be tempted to pin all of this on their interpretations
of Scripture, that they either misunderstood it or, more fundamentally, misunderstood the nature and function of Scripture. While
I certainly believe they failed to understand Scripture in a very
fundamental way, I suspect this is better understood as a symptom
than cause of their problem.

That said, symptoms can easily become a part of our problem
and must sometimes be managed before we can get diagnostically
to the deeper pathologies. For this reason and others, our first task
is to consider what these confused souls may have misunderstood
about Scripture. We must consider the nature of the Bible, of what it
is and, as an implication, of what it *isn't*. The philosophers among us
would say that we must consider the *ontology* of Scripture.

1. Augustine 1887b:533.

About the Nature of Scripture

The Jewish and Christian traditions have generally maintained that the Bible is wholly different from other books. In one way or another, it was written by God and hence was produced in a way that shielded it from the error and foibles of the humans who penned the text. This was accomplished through divine "inspiration," an English word behind which we find various Hebrew, Aramaic, and Greek concepts, of which the best known among Christians is the Greek word *theopneustos*, meaning "god-breathed" (2 Tim 3:16).[2] As a result, Scripture is often described not only as "authoritative" but also as "inerrant" or "infallible" or some related concept that supports its authority. This seems very reasonable, for if God, by definition, does not err, then it follows that God does not err in Scripture. The Bible is thus construed, in the nature of the case, as the "final authority" for matters of faith and faithful practice and even, in some circles, for any and all matters apparently addressed in it. This outcome is almost inevitable because our ideas about the nature of Scripture tend to strongly influence our response to the text (Webster 2003:5).

Although Jews and Christians have generally thought about the Bible like this, the apparent complexity of Holy Scripture has not gone unnoticed over the centuries. The Fathers of the early Church often resolved the apparent tensions and contradictions in the Bible by using an allegorical approach, as did some Jewish interpreters, but this and related approaches remained within the traditional frame of reference. Things began to change in the seventeenth century, however. From that point forward, beginning more or less with the Jewish scholar, Baruch Spinoza, serious questions were raised about biblical authority within the Jewish and Christian traditions (Spinoza 1640; Preus 2001). Spinoza pointed out, for example, that Moses taught an "eye-for-an-eye" response to violence whereas Jesus (in contrast) instructed his disciples to "turn the other cheek." Based on this and many similar

---

2. For brief discussions, see Greenberger 1997 [Judaism] and Webster 2005 [Christianity].

examples from Scripture, Spinoza argued that the biblical canon, when studied carefully, turns out to be an historically contingent document with many different viewpoints. It is really no different from any other book we might read.

If I may be so bold as to skip forward for convenience to our own twenty-first-century context, it is obvious to all of us (I assume) that many Jews and Christians now agree with Spinoza to an extent and have some or many doubts about the authority of the Bible. Over the course of four centuries, the skeptics have added to Spinoza's list of apparent problems not only more contradictions within the Bible but also new conflicts between the Bible and the larger world, especially with respect to the historical and scientific evidence. These issues need to be explored and hopefully sorted out to an extent in our discussion.

Commonly, the different views of Scripture and theology are described with labels like "conservative" and "progressive" and "moderate" and "liberal," monikers borne with honor by some and used as pejorative criticism by others. Some people don't mind these kinds of labels and others do, especially on an assumption that labels generate stereotypes rather than promote understanding. For the purposes of this essay, I will try to bypass these conventional labels by using two others which, I hope, are less loaded with ideological and political baggage.

Let us suppose, for the sake of discussion, that there are two basic Christian views of the Bible. One approach views the Bible as basically divine (but also human), and the other views the Bible as basically human (but also divine). In the first approach, the Bible is so much a product of God's initiative that it can only yield words that suit God's character as an omniscient, omnipotent, inerrant deity. From Genesis to Revelation, every page of Scripture agrees with every other page, and the whole of it has been insulated by God from the errors and foibles of the human authors who penned it. The brokenness and darkness of the human soul is described, confronted, and healed in this kind of Bible, but never does the Bible condone or advance these human traits. If this is the Bible we have, then it would be unique as the only theological book in our possession that's completely accurate in every respect.

The other approach, the human-but-also-divine approach, views the Bible as so much a product of human initiative that it cannot help but reflect the limitations and brokenness of the human condition. On this view of Scripture, God did not use the human authors to pass the "pure divine word" from heaven to earth but rather accepted as Scripture what they wrote on the basis of their relationship to and understanding of God. We may say that these authors were "inspired," as Scripture does, but this will not mean they wrote only from the divine viewpoint. Rather, they wrote as people influenced by God but wholly from their perspectives as finite, broken human beings. In this understanding of Scripture, the Bible is informed by God's activity but nevertheless speaks from the moral and perceptual limitations of its human authors and audience. It can be trusted in the way that a good friend can be trusted. Good friends are dependable and we always listen to them, but they are not perfect and can make mistakes.

For the sake of convenience, I will refer to these two views as the *foundational* and the *contextual* views of Scripture. The *foundational* view holds that Scripture, as our only perfect theological book, provides an utterly unique foundation for Christian theology. Because it is without error, Scripture is the lens through which all other evidence is properly viewed, not only in matters of theology but also, because of this, in all matters that might touch on theology, such as astronomy, biology, psychology, history, anthropology, sociology, ethics, politics, economics, and any other area of study that claims to say something about humanity and the human condition. Thus, for example, the foundationalist will reject the scientific evidence for an ancient earth if he believes, on the basis of Genesis, that the earth is only a few thousand years old.

The *contextual* view takes a different view of things, for it assumes that the human authors of Scripture, though selected to write on God's behalf, wrote from and in relation to their limited human horizons. What they wrote is important but humanly imperfect, so we are wise, when reading and applying any biblical text, to seek further counsel from other biblical texts and also from the broader fruit of human inquiry. In other words, the contextual view is contextual in two respects. It considers the Bible to be the contingent product of human beings who were formed in and spoke from concrete social contexts, and it takes very seriously any evidence from the larger world (or context) to which the biblical text must ultimately relate. To return to my previous example, a contextualist might agree that Genesis teaches about a "young earth" but allow, on the basis of current science, that it is actually billions of years old. She will assume that the biblical author got this wrong because he lived before the era of scientific geology and astronomy. God does not make mistakes, but human beings can and do make them.

I am *very* aware that my descriptions of these approaches will strike some readers as caricatures of theology, which paint the two sides in ham-fisted simplicity and leave out other views besides. Certainly there are other views on this subject, and certainly each of these approaches could be described with more thoughtful nuance and intellectual subtlety than I have provided here. But when all is considered, I would argue that, amongst Christians who accept the Bible as God's written word, these are essentially our two options: either the Bible is so divine that it has been protected from the error and vice of its humanity, or God has permitted a Bible so human that it includes human error and vice.

Furthermore, when we speak of theoretical approaches like Foundationalism and Contextualism, we should keep in mind that, in the nature of the case, we are referring primarily to the "thought leaders" who espouse these viewpoints rather than the proverbial church-pew Christian. The average Christian may never have considered these issues in any detail and has probably inherited a view of Scripture from the general habits and assumptions of their Church tradition. This does not mean that the lectures have no relevance for the average Christian; they certainly have relevance, precisely because the average Christian has not thought much about it. Over the last few centuries, we have managed with astounding success to expand humanity's access to the Bible. Billions of people now have one or more copies in their possession.

But have we adequately prepared these billions to responsibly read and apply the Bible to the concrete circumstances of their social and cultural contexts? One of my assumptions in these lectures is that we have not done this well. In what follows, I hope to address not only the needs of Christian "thought leaders" but also of the average Christian who simply wants to read and apply the Bible in a way that honors their allegiance to God.

To return to our main theme, the two views of Scripture, let us consider together each of them, attending carefully to their respective advantages and disadvantages and to the facts and evidence as well as these can be assessed. And as a matter of humility, let us keep in mind what we have learned from the story of Job, that no human viewpoint can fully represent God's view of things. We can only advance towards rather than arrive at the right destination. In the end, we should expect no better outcome than was achieved by Job, who finally repented in dust and ashes. That this was his response can remind us that our discussion, while a matter of academic and intellectual inquiry, is also a matter of spiritual and ethical formation. Job's friends and the Pharisees were uncharitable, in part, because of their false views of Holy Scripture.

The Foundational View of Scripture

Christians have written thousands and thousands of books on Scripture, addressing its various parts in terms of language, history, and interpretation, and also exploring key theological issues related to it, such as inspiration, authority, and revelation. I cannot hope in these short essays to honor sufficiently all of these capable authors, but I shall endeavor (as best I can) to take them into account as our discussion moves on. For the sake of the conversation, however, I have selected one ancient Christian scholar to provide a touchstone for the lectures.

Of the early Christian Fathers, Augustine (AD 354–430) is perhaps the most accredited in the eyes of the ecumenical church.[3]

---

3. Augustine was the Bishop of Hippo, in what is now the modern town of Annaba, Algeria.

He is especially revered within the Catholic tradition but respected also within the Eastern Orthodox and Protestant communities. Although Bishop Augustine's best known work is undoubtedly *De civitate Dei*, "the City of God," towards the end of his life he produced a brief but outstanding treatise on the interpretation of the Bible. It is to this short work, entitled *De Doctrina Christiana* or "On Christian Doctrine," that I shall refer from time to time in the lectures (Augustine 1887b). I have read this piece at least a dozen times and am struck, every time, by the remarkable prescience of Augustine, in that he so often touched on the key issues that still confront biblical scholars and theologians to this day. Respecting his doctrine of Scripture, Augustine is best described as a biblical foundationalist, but his observations about the Bible, and his resulting suggestions, often foreshadowed the theological strategies used by modern contextualists. I do not always agree with Augustine, nor, perhaps, will you. But I've found him to be a trusted and dependable friend on the Christian journey.

The foundationalist viewpoint claims, as its chief advantage, that it secures "the truth" in a diverse and complicated world. With such a Bible, we are not driven this way and that by the shifting tides of culture but rather stand on a solid foundation, which points us not only to the right behaviors but also to a secure relationship with God. Jesus Christ, embraced by all Christians as God's solution for the human condition, is known to us as a historical person and teacher almost wholly through the four gospels and other New Testament reflections on his life. We have learned from these documents about the darkness of the human soul, about God's sacrificial love for humanity, and about the resources that God has given us to pursue love for our neighbor, including even our enemies. Some biblical concepts, like "do unto others" and the "Good Samaritan," are so compelling that not only Christians but just about everyone embraces them as good and healthy. Scripture further attests to God's ongoing relationship with Christians and the Church, especially but not only through the activity of the Holy Spirit. And best of all, Scripture protects us from anxieties about the afterlife. We can know for sure that God loves us and that we will be saved. The foundational view of Scripture is very common and convincing because it connects so organically to what Christians have discovered is important for human and spiritual health.

The foundational viewpoint is supported by specific texts from both the Old and New Testaments, which together suggest that God was active in the creation of Scripture and, because of this, that the result would be a perfect expression of the divine word.

> The law of the LORD is perfect, reviving the soul;
>> The decrees of the LORD are sure, making wise the simple;
> the precepts of the LORD are right, rejoicing the heart;
>> the commandment of the LORD is clear, enlightening the eyes (Ps 19:7–8)

> The LORD exists forever;
>> your word is firmly fixed in heaven. (Ps 119:89)

> Every word of God is pure. (Prov 30:5a)

> All scripture is inspired by God and is useful for teaching, for reproof, for correction, and for training in righteousness, so that everyone who belongs to God may be proficient, equipped for every good work. (2 Tim 3:16–17)

> We also constantly give thanks to God for this, that when you received the word of God that you heard from us, you accepted it not as a human word but as what it really is, God's word, which is also at work in you believers. (1 Thess 2:13)

> First of all you must understand this, that no prophecy of scripture is a matter of one's own interpretation, because no prophecy ever came by human will, but men moved by the Holy Spirit spoke from God. (2 Pet 2:20–21)

Many biblical texts advance the more general point that God is perfect and truthful, virtues that according to Christian philosophy are proper to God by definition.[4] The foundationalist will infer

4. A classic argument for God's goodness and truth appeared in the

from this, apparently for good reasons, that any human errors in Scripture would imply that God is less than perfect or that, in the end, the Bible is not really God's word at all.

Foundationalism's optimistic belief in the reliability of Scripture is further supported by the many goods found in it, including those earlier mentioned, such as love for God and neighbor (including our enemies) and others that could be summed up as "fruits of the Spirit" (Gal 5:22–23). That so many Christians believe the foundational view, including even many trained scholars, is only possible because so much in Scripture is good, true, and beautiful.

The foundational view also has as an advantage its long-standing pedigree, that it has been, more or less, the standard view of things among Jews and Christians for most of their respective religious histories. Augustine expressed it this way 1600 years ago: "Now faith will totter if the authority of Scripture begins to shake. And then, if faith totters, love itself will grow cold" (Augustine 1887b:533).[5] In other words, if the foundation of Scripture is lost, so is our access to love for God and neighbor. It is a sentiment expressed by theologians throughout Christian history. Why abandon this tried and tested dogma? "The proof is in the pudding," as they say, and the foundational approach has proved its value for centuries of believers and, in the view of foundationalists, for those living today.

All of this is to say: the foundationalist view of Scripture is supported by significant evidence from Scripture, tradition, and experience. For these reasons and others I'll not mention at this point, it has long been and still is accepted as the correct view by most who sit in the proverbial church pew.

We will consider the alternative view, the contextual view, in the next lecture. But before we do, several additional comments are in order about Foundationalism.

---

thirteenth-century work of Aquinas, in his *Summa Theologica*, part 1, questions 6 and 16 (see Aquinas 1981:1.28–30, 92–93).

5. I have slightly adjusted the translation to suit modern English convention.

First, my (presumably) American audience will perhaps draw a direct line between the historical Foundationalism just described and more "literal" approaches to the Bible now popular within the Fundamentalist and Evangelical communities of the United States. While there is certainly a relationship here, the approach of conservative American theology, which developed over the last century or so, is not only diverse in itself but also one of the many "biblical Foundationalisms" embraced by Christians over the course of two-thousand years. I will try to draw out these distinctions in the next few paragraphs.

Second, biblical Foundationalism took a particular turn during the Reformation and by this diverged significantly from Foundationalism as generally understood during the previous sixteen centuries. While earlier foundationalists assumed the Bible was and is a perfect book, they were comfortable admitting that our interpretations are by no means certain. Augustine (1882:753) speaks to this in *On Christian Doctrine*, where he describes the threat posed when we embrace with certainty a false understanding of Scripture. Nothing is quite as dangerous as confidently being wrong. But the Reformers were very (very) confident, nonetheless. The reason is easy to understand.

To support their struggle against Catholic authority, men like Luther, Calvin, Cranmer, and Arminius needed much more than a dependable Bible; they needed a *perspicuous* Bible, which yielded clear and obvious meanings to the reader of Scripture. Anything less would mean that human beings can't really know, when they read the Bible, whether they're actually hearing the word of God or only warped echoes of their own mind. For the reasons just outlined, the Protestant tradition to this day depends, more or less, on this perfect and perspicuous Bible. This is particularly true of the Fundamentalist and Evangelical Christian traditions in America, where lay Bible reading is such an important part of faith and doctrine. All of this is somewhat less important within Catholic and Orthodox Foundationalisms, where Church tradition rather than Scripture alone provides the final authority in matters of theology.

Third, because of their confidence in Scripture and also to preserve this confidence, foundationalist theologians have often labored to solve the apparent conflicts found in its pages. We will consider four of the most common strategies used by these scholars just below, but we should note that, in general, foundationalists often proceed in their theological work as if the problems do not exist. I suspect that in many cases they simply don't notice the difficulties, but I am also aware of instances in which the problems are avoided intentionally.[6] Whether this last strategy is appropriate or not depends, I suppose, on the context and audience of the writer.

Harmonizations

When Christians assume that the Bible is a perfect book and yet find within it apparent discrepancies and contradictions, the most natural and common response is to infer that these are illusions and that, in the end, what is said in one place is really the same as in another. Consider, for example, the two biblical accounts of the death of Judas. In Matthew's account, Judas commits suicide and dies by hanging, while in Luke's account, in Acts, he apparently dies in an accidental fall, causing his body to "burst open" (cf. Matt 27:3–8; Acts 1:18–19). There are other striking differences in the two stories, but let's confine ourselves to this one. What should the foundationalist do with this apparent contradiction?

Within the Christian exegetical history, two solutions have often been proposed. One holds that after Judas hung himself, his dead body sooner or later fell to the ground.[7] Another solution, very ancient and more ingenious I'd say, holds that Judas failed at suicide by hanging and later died in a fall, as described by Luke.[8]

6. One Evangelical scholar admitted to me that he skipped a problematic passage in his commentary on Ezekiel because he did not know how to manage the "failed" prophecy it contained (see the relevant prophecies on Tyre in Ezek 26:7–21; 29:18–20).

7. As noted by Fitzmyer 1998:224.

8. This is a very old solution, which appears already in the second century commentary of Papias (2003:105) and in the eleventh-century commentary of

These solutions originated in antiquity and are still accepted in some circles, but most modern foundationalists, particularly those well trained, are reluctant to accept dramatic harmonizations of the kind just described. Donald Carson (1984:562), a well-known Evangelical scholar, assumes that a harmonization must exist but refreshingly admits there is no clear path to reach it.

The Spiritual Sense of Scripture

For much of Church history, the contradictions in Scripture have been resolved by appealing to the spiritual rather than the literal meaning of the text. Saint Gregory (sixth century) described this approach as well as anyone: "Undoubtedly the words of the literal text, when they do not agree with each other, show that something else is to be sought in them. It is as if they said to us, 'When you see us apparently embarrassed and contradictory, look within us for that which is coherent and consistent'" (Gregory 2004:89). A common patristic approach assumed that a given text could have four levels of meaning, including the literal, allegorical, tropological, and anagogical meanings (see Steinmetz 1980).[9] While modern readers may find some of the patristic solutions a bit fanciful, they were inspired by the Apostle Paul's comment that "the letter kills, but the Spirit gives life" (2 Cor 3:6).

Accommodation

Another old strategy, perhaps more appealing to modern readers, asserts that the biblical authors, where they seem to err, were in fact only assuming the mistaken views of their naive audience. A good example of this approach is found in John Calvin's sixteenth-century commentary on Genesis. As the reader may know, the

---

Theophylact (1992).

9. The adjective "patristic" refers to the earliest scholars of the Christian church, dating from the New Testament to about the seventh century AD. For accessible introductions, see Hall 1998; 2002.

biblical creation story (Gen 1) asserts that there are "waters above the firmament," which even in Calvin's day could not be squared with accepted science. About this, the Reformer wrote:

> For, to my mind, this is a certain principle: that nothing is treated here except the visible form of the world. Whoever wishes to learn astronomy and other esoteric arts, let him go elsewhere ... Therefore, the things which he [i.e., Moses] relates, serve as the garniture of that theatre which he [i.e., God] places before our eyes. From this I conclude that the waters intended here are such as the crude and unlearned may perceive. The assertion of some, that they embrace by faith what they have read concerning the waters above the heavens, notwithstanding their ignorance of them, is not in accordance with the design of Moses. And truly a longer inquiry into a matter open and manifest is superfluous. (Calvin 1847:1.79–80)

One should not believe by "faith" (says Calvin) that there are waters above the heavens when one knows good and well that this is not the case. Genesis merely accommodated itself to the ancient view that such waters existed. Calvin describes this approach to Scripture more clearly in his *Institutes*:

> For who is so devoid of intellect as not to understand that God, in so speaking, lisps with us as nurses are wont to do with little children? Such modes of expression, therefore, do not so much express what kind of a being God is, as accommodate the knowledge of him to our feebleness. In doing so, he must, of course, stoop far below his proper height. (Calvin 1949:1.110)[10]

Let us be clear: Calvin always worked hard to resolve the apparent contradictions and tensions that he found in the Bible. But when this effort failed—and sometimes it did—he was not above admitting that something errant appeared in the pages of Scripture. For these kinds of difficulties, Calvin tells us that whenever the Bible appears to speak "falsely," this reflects an accommodation to the

---

10. For more on Calvin's use of accommodation, see Wright 1986; Greene-McCreight 1999; Balserak 2002.

false views of humanity. Many Jews and Christians, living both before and after Calvin, have employed the same hermeneutical strategy (Benin 1993).

Literary Genre

We noted above, in our discussion of the "Spiritual Meaning of Scripture," that Christians have sometimes resolved the apparent problems in the Bible by appealing to genre. If the literal text troubles us, then perhaps the genre is something else, such as an allegory. This is the idea. What the Fathers of the Church did with their four-fold meaning of the text anticipated generic approaches that have become very common and much more sophisticated among modern foundationalists.

From the nineteenth century onward, ancient texts and artifacts were discovered in the Near East that dramatically widened our perspective of the world of ancient Israel and the first Christians (see Sparks 2005; Evans 2005). Some of these non-biblical "pagan" texts, such as the Sumerian and Babylonian Flood stories, were very similar to the biblical traditions and spawned within biblical Foundationalism a whole new tradition of scholarship. Foundationalists surmised that in many cases the Bible appears to include errors because we have wrongly read it through our modern lens rather than through the lenses of its ancient authors and audiences. Let us consider an example.

We noted already, in the first lecture, that the four gospels include some striking differences that appear to be contradictions. What if these differences were artistic embellishments rather than historical errors? Robert Gundry made such an argument in 1982, when he suggested that the gospel of Matthew diverges from the other Synoptics, Mark and Luke, because Matthew was written using a Jewish exegetical method called midrash.[11] This would mean (says Gundry) that Matthew did not write a poor biography of Jesus but rather a very artistic, theological story about him. We

---

11. For an introduction to midrash, see Strack and Stemberger 1992: 254–393.

needn't agree with Gundry to see his point. If the biblical authors wrote according to ancient rather than modern standards of precision and accuracy, then perhaps we should not foist upon them our modern canons of perfection. What appear to be "errors" may in fact be something else altogether.

In a philosophical twist on literary genre, some foundationalists have argued that each biblical text is a "speech act" and that only this intentional act, rather than any contextual assumptions made in it, should be evaluated in terms of accuracy or error.[12] Walton and Sandy (2013:49–59) have suggested, for example, that neither God nor the human authors of Scripture intended, by their speech acts, to reveal new facts about science in the Bible. It follows that the biblical writers should not be criticized when their science is, let us say, less than perfect. One can find a very sophisticated case for the speech-act approach to Scripture in Kevin Vanhoozer's book, *Is There a Meaning in This Text?* (1998).

I will simply add here that, in my view, the more one sees the need for these interpretive strategies, the closer one comes to the alternative, contextual approach.

Summary: Biblical Foundationalism

The case for biblical Foundationalism is based on Scripture, tradition, and experience, and has been supported, where it seems weak, by several well-tested exegetical and theological strategies, both ancient and modern. We must now consider whether this body of evidence, as convincing as it may seem, is truer to the facts than the contextual alternative.

12. For the philosophical background, see Austin 1962; Alston 1964; 2000; Searle 1969.

——— *Lecture Three* ———

What Is the Bible?

The Contextual Approach

*"It is a disgraceful and dangerous thing for an infidel to
hear a Christian, presumably giving the meaning of Holy
Scripture, talking nonsense on these topics."*

—St. Augustine[1]

*"We must read this book of books with all human methods.
But through the fragile and broken Bible, God meets us in
the voice of the Risen One."*

—Dietrich Bonhoeffer[2]

Let us consider the contextual view in roughly the reverse order
of the points just made in favor of biblical Foundationalism.
And let us note, from the outset, that many contextualists accept, in
principle, the interpretive strategies of the foundationalists outlined
just above. Harmonization is a natural tool when our sources do
not match precisely, and the notion that Scripture includes not only
literal but also spiritual and allegorical meanings is also a common
if not standard viewpoint in the guild. Accommodation, or some
facsimile thereof, is essentially implied if we accept that the Bible
is (or includes) a humanly finite expression of things divine. And
respecting modern approaches to the literary genres of Scripture,

1. Augustine 1982:1.42–43.
2. Bonhoeffer 2004:15.

which try to read them as ancient rather than modern texts, this is not only accepted but applauded by most contextualist scholars; the same is true of philosophical approaches to Scripture.

Contextualists argue, however, that the tools just listed, however important and helpful, do not deliver a perfect Bible. The literary genres of Scripture appear to be much more human than the foundationalists believe, in part because they are so similar to the ancient "pagan" texts and in part because the ancient documents and artifacts frequently reveal gaffes in the biblical history (see Sparks 2005; 2008). Accommodation, in the nature of the case, is necessary only because we're already admitting that genuine problems appear in the text. As for the harmonizations and allegories, these must have reasonable limits or we'll end up with solutions that only the very gullible can believe. One gets the impression that these strategies are necessary only because biblical Foundationalism has misunderstood the Bible in the first place.

But the contextualist objections to Foundationalism are more basic and practical than all this. Contextualists point out that Foundationalism, in spite of its bold claim to provide a firm basis for the truth, does not actually provide this fixed foundation. The meaning of Scripture, for example, turns out to be far from clear. Christian denominations number in the thousands and biblical interpretations in the millions, despite the fact that most of them appeal to readings from a perfect Bible. One finds among the committed foundationalists those who believe in "predestination" and "free will," in "premillennial" and "postmillennial" eschatology, in "infant baptism" and "believer's baptism," and in "elder rule" and "congregational rule." And more importantly, these groups often have very different views about how human beings can be "saved." On almost every important interpretive question in every biblical book, we find a wide variety of "perfect" readings. So it is clear that Foundationalism does not guarantee a correct reading of Scripture, nor does it prevent all sorts of exegetical tomfoolery. Some modern cult groups are biblical foundationalists.

In a related matter, which we will explore here at length, Christianity has struggled through much of its history to reconcile a perfect Bible with the "hard facts" of science. As early as the fifth century, Augustine warned Christians to avoid twisting the scientific evidence so as to make it fit their view of Scripture:

> It is a disgraceful and dangerous thing for an infidel to hear a Christian, presumably giving the meaning of Holy Scripture, talking nonsense on these topics; and we should take all means to prevent such an embarrassing situation, in which people show up vast ignorance in a Christian and laugh it to scorn. (Augustine 1982:1:42–43)

We don't know what scientific issues Augustine had in mind, but the Church has struggled during its history to accept loads of science, including (but not limited to) the spherical shape of the earth, the heliocentric view of the solar system, the geological and astronomical ages of the earth and cosmos, the evolutionary origins of humanity, and the neuroscience of religion (White 1896; Brooke 1991; Green and Palmer 2005; Polkinghorne 2009).

Christian debates about astronomy during the sixteenth and seventeenth centuries provide a striking example of the Church/ science schism because we can view them with the benefit of hindsight. The standard view during this period was the Ptolemaic view, that the earth stood at the center of the universe with the Sun, moon, planets, and stars revolving around it. Copernicus (1473–1543) and later Galileo (1564–1642) proffered an alternative theory, which held on the contrary that the earth was circling the sun. This theory met with sharp resistance both among the magisterial reformers and eventually within the Catholic Church.[3]

Catholic authorities did not immediately respond to Copernicus, but the reformers did. Luther (1483–1546) referred to Copernicus as an "upstart astrologer" and as a "fool [who] wishes to reverse the entire science of astronomy; but sacred Scripture tells us that Joshua commanded the sun to stand still, and not the earth"

---

3. For discussions of Copernicus, see Hagen 1908; Kuhn 1957; Gingerich and MacLachlan 2005; White 1896; for Galileo, see De Santillana 1955; Machamer 1998; Langford 2003.

(White 1896:1.126).[4] Luther's associate Melanchthon (1497–1560) added these words of criticism:

> The eyes are witnesses that the heavens revolve in the space of twenty-four hours. But certain men, either from the love of novelty, or to make a display of ingenuity, have concluded that the earth moves . . . Now, it is a want of honesty and decency to assert such notions publicly, and the example is pernicious. It is the part of a good mind to accept the truth as revealed by God and to acquiesce in it. (White 1896:1.126–27)[5]

Melanchthon believed that wise governments ought to "repress" the views of Copernicus because "public proclamation of absurd opinions is indecent and sets a harmful example." In support of this opinion, he could cite biblical texts such as Eccl 1:5: "The sun rises and the sun goes down, and hastens to the place where it rises." John Calvin (1509–1564) seems to have mostly ignored Copernicus, but his biblical commentaries assume the Ptolemaic view,[6] and in at least one case he offered a scathing critique of the Copernican astronomy:

> We will see some who are so deranged, not only in religion but who in all things reveal their monstrous nature, that they will say that the sun does not move, and that it is the earth which shifts and turns. When we see such minds we must indeed confess that the devil possesses them, and that God sets them before us as mirrors, in order to keep us in his fear . . . When they are told: "That is hot," they will reply: "No, it is plainly cold." When they are shown an object that is black, they will say that it is white, or vice versa. (White 1980: 236)[7]

Calvin says elsewhere that the Bible should not be used as an astronomy textbook,[8] but he seems not to have applied his insight

4. White's translation from the German: Luther 1880–1910:22.1546.
5. White's translation from the Latin: Melanchthon 1846:212–20.
6. See, for example, his comments on Ps 93:1 in Calvin 1845:4.6–7.
7. White's translation from the French: Calvin 1846:677.
8. In Calvin's comments on Gen 1:5–6, 16 (Calvin 1847:1.77–80, 86–87),

to this problem, perhaps because the new theory contravened common sense. Calvin, Luther, and Melanchthon are merely representative of general trends in the sixteenth century, in which clergymen feverishly searched the Bible line by line for new passages that would confirm the traditional Ptolemaic view.

As I said, the Catholic authorities did not immediately attend to the work of Copernicus. But about seventy years later, they arrested, tried, and convicted Galileo for similar scientific views. He was put under house arrest for life and his books were banned, not only those existing but also the publication of any future books. It was in this context that the older works of Copernicus were censored to remove from them any content that would overtly support Galileo (Hagen 1908). The Church did not fully accept its error and lift these bans until the eighteenth century in the case of Copernicus (Hagen 1908) and the nineteenth century for Galileo (Langford 2003).

If we apply a bit of imagination to the past, it is easy to see why the Reformers and Catholics took these hard-line positions against Copernicus and Galileo. First, the Ptolemaic view was matched step for step by the long-standing traditions of the Church. Second, the Ptolemaic view corresponded rather precisely to the usual experiences of human life—that the sun is moving and we are not. And third, as we have just seen, the geocentric view had Scripture on its side. Tradition, common sense, and the voice of Scripture joined together to create a coherent understanding of the world against which the Copernican viewpoint seemed senseless, even heretical. Ultimately, however, the Copernican viewpoint would win the day. The reason, of course, was that the scientific evidence finally coalesced into a consensus against which tradition, Scripture, and common sense could no longer prevail.

I raise the examples of Copernicus and Galileo because the Church in some sectors is still making the same kinds of mistakes. Christian foundationalists in our own day (who believe in a perfect Bible) are far more likely to stand against scientifically accredited views of astronomy, biology, neuroscience, geology, and

and Ps 136:7 (Calvin 1845:5.184).

the environment than the average person. And if this is how they respond to hard scientific evidence, the threat of error is greater still when the subject to be considered cannot be studied with hard evidence, as is true when we're considering moral, ethical, and spiritual questions. I will discuss this problem later in the lectures. At any rate, this is why contextualists believe that Foundationalism doesn't work as well as the foundationalists believe. Foundationalists are committed in a particular way to a particular kind of Bible, and this ultimately prevents them from taking seriously the non-biblical information available to humanity.

Contextualists find further support for their view of Scripture within the Bible itself, in that some texts stand in tension not only with known science but also with other texts in the collection. We noted earlier that the Bible offers two entirely different stories about how Judas the disciple died. According to the contextualists, this is merely a facile example of a pervasive feature in Scripture. We will need to consider this issue straight away, but first a bit of preparation is in order for my foundationalist readers.

One of the fathers of modern psychology, William James (1902:9), was right when he said that "we instinctively recoil from seeing an object to which our emotions and affections are committed handled by the intellect as any other object is handled." And I can think of no case when this is truer than when our holy book is so treated. As we review in the next few paragraphs the diversity of Scripture, including its possible tensions and contradictions, I do not intend at all to impugn the biblical authors, their books, or God. If they erred, they err as we all do. And if they erred, it was their weakness and not God's that is behind it. So again, I mean no harm in what comes next. But the road to hell is (as they say) paved with good intentions, and I realize that some Christians are inevitably troubled, perhaps even filled with righteous anger, when anyone suggests that the Bible is somewhat less divine than it might be. I can understand this response. And if this exercise engenders in the reader such an experience, I apologize in advance for the effect. My purpose is to pursue the truth of theology rather than to create angst and theological confusion.

Let us consider now a list of what appear to be "tensions" and "contradictions" within Scripture. I admit that the list is fairly long, but this is a necessary exercise if the point is to be appreciated. One or a few apparent "contradictions" can be easily explained within the foundational model as rare exceptions to the rule and thus, it is assumed, as "optical illusions" rather than actual problems. If the alternative view of the contextualists is to be considered honestly, we must ask with seriousness whether these illusions are actually rare or are, instead, so common that they are evidence of a real rather than imaginary problem. So let us begin.

The Bible includes hundreds of texts that provide conflicting messages. Some texts depict God changing his[9] mind and others claim that God never changes (Gen 6:6–7; Jas 1:17). Some texts describe God as having a physical body and others strongly assert that he does not have a body (Isa 6:1; Amos 9:1; John 4:24). Some texts say that Israel's forefathers knew God's name, Yahweh, and others explicitly claim that they did not know his name (Gen 28:16; Exod 6:2–3). One text says that God's people should boil the Passover meal and another forbids boiling it (Deut 16:7; Exod 12:9). Some texts permitted Israel to sacrifice at many places before Solomon's temple was built, while others do not permit this (Deut 12:8–14; Lev 17:8–9). There are texts that promise judgment on the children of sinners, and those that say God certainly does not harm children for the sins of their parents (Exod 20:5; Deut 24:16). Some texts direct God's people to divorce unbelieving spouses, and others say that we certainly should not divorce them (Ezra 9–10; 1 Cor 7:10–16).

We have a text that says Jesus' family was originally from Nazareth, and another that says they were from Bethlehem (Luke 2:1–4; Matt 1–2); in a related matter, we have a text that says Jesus moved to Nazareth soon after his birth and also a text that says this happened several years later (Luke 2:39–40; Matt 1–2). We have a

---

9. The gender of God is neither male nor female, so I have attempted as much as possible to avoid referring to the deity with pronouns. But where the effect would be stilted, I have nonetheless retained the traditional masculine form.

text that says that idol worshippers are without excuse, but another that excuses them (Rom 1:18–23; Acts 17:29–31).

One text says that David was an adulterer and murderer, and another portrays him as wholly righteous and innocent (2 Sam 11–12; cf. 1 Chr). One text says King David paid fifty shekels of silver for Israel's temple site, and another that he paid 600 shekels of gold (2 Sam 24:24; 1 Chr 21:25). We have a text that says the world will inevitably hate Christians, and another that encourages Christians to pursue peace with all people (John 15:18–21; Heb 12:14). We have a text that claims God is not willing for anyone to perish, and another that seems to say he has predestined some human beings to eternal judgment (2 Pet 3:9; Rom 9:1–24).

On the scientific front, the Bible ostensibly indicates the earth is a few thousand years old, yet science tells us that it is billions of years old. The Bible says that human beings were created on day 6 of a six-day creation process, and science tells us human beings were created through a complex evolutionary process that took millions of years. The Bible claims that there was a worldwide flood that killed almost every living thing, while the geological and biological evidence proves that this never happened.

This long list of texts is in fact a very small sample of the phenomenon under consideration, in which the biblical authors offer conflicting viewpoints on history, facts, and perspectives.[10] That one foundationalist found it necessary to produce an "encyclopedia" to address the issue illustrates the extent of this evidence (Archer 1982).

The issues listed so far have concerned matters of fact and perspective, but there are other problems in Scripture of greater significance for theology and with more potential impact on Christian living. I will illustrate this by citing one text from the biblical laws in Exodus:

> When a man strikes his slave, male or female, with a rod
> and the slave dies under his hand, he shall be punished.

10. One can find many other examples by reading a synoptic harmony of the Old Testament histories or of the New Testament gospels, such as Newsome 1986 and Swanson 1984.

But if the slave survives a day or two, he is not to be pun-
ished; for the slave is his money. (Exod 21:20–21)[11]

The Israelite slave owner is permitted by the law to own and beat
his slave, and not only to beat him but to beat him until he is nearly
dead. And should he actually die, the slave owner faces no further
consequence beyond the immediate consequence, which is that
he has lost a man or woman for whom he has already paid out
money. The law perhaps had its positive side, in that it honored
to an extent the humanity of the slave and may have represented
at the time a step forward in slave rights (Cassuto 1967:270–71),
but it falls well short of the ethical gospel as taught by Jesus Christ.
Jesus taught about loving every person, including our enemies,
and entreated his disciples to "Do unto others as you'd have done
to you." Only by contortions of a strange kind can we claim that
this law conforms to the golden rule. My guess is that most readers
have never noticed this biblical law and are a bit unnerved to learn
that it sits within the same Bible as John 3:16.

The law just cited is not exceptional within the Old Testament.
Many biblical laws (and other texts) assume and even reinforce
the power and privilege of some people over others, particularly of
men over women, of Israelites over foreigners, and of free persons
over slaves. But the matter under consideration is not limited to
only discrete texts but in fact extends to the proverbial "warp and
woof" (the fabric) of the Old Testament narrative.

According to the book of Deuteronomy, the Israelites were
commanded by God to invade the land of Canaan and kill all of its
inhabitants, including not only the fighting men but also the old,
women, and children; even the animals were to be killed (Deut
7; cf. Deut 2:34; 3:6). The law specifically warns them against
"showing mercy" (Deut 7:2), as if to say: "Should you look your
enemy in the eye and notice their humanity, do not let your heart

---

11. Citing here the RSV. This translation reflects the standard translation
and commentary tradition as found in Hebrew, Aramaic, Greek, Latin, Luther,
Calvin, and the major English translations, from the KJV to NRSV. The only exception is NIV, a translation prepared by foundationalists, which attempts (un-
successfully in my view) to reduce the tensions between the law and the gospel.

be moved. They must be killed." This command is construed in Hebrew as a formal sacrifice, called a *hērem*, in which all of the people and possessions of the conquered land are given over to Yahweh. The reader will probably know that the prescribed attack on Canaan was immediately carried out in the book of Joshua, where we find that obedience to the slaughter law yielded God's blessings and success, whereas disobedience led to God's curses and trouble (cf. Josh 6–8).

While the scale of this *hērem* law is much broader than the slave law we discussed just above, the basic problem is the same. In both texts, God seems to command his people, Israel, to behave in ways that run counter to the gospel of love as taught by Jesus Christ. This is, at least, how contextual approaches to the Bible see the situation. In other words, contextualists will want to say (in fact, by definition need to say) that God did not actually command the Israelites to kill the Canaanites nor did God endorse the freedom of slave owners to beat their slaves. Rather, the Israelites justified for themselves these darker behaviors by cloaking them in the guise of divine law.

This theological and exegetical move illustrates well the basic claim of the contextual approach, that the Bible is the product of profoundly human social contexts. And if this is the case, then Christians must attend not only to the contextual situations that produced the biblical text but also to the larger context of the biblical canon. When one biblical text stands in tension or conflict with another, a choice must be made about which text presents the clearer picture of God and healthy Christian behavior. Contextualists will hold that Jesus has in fact provided us with a template for this theological decision when he said that the whole of Scripture hangs from the dictum, "Love God, and love your neighbor" (Matt 22:24–40). Thus, when a "text of terror" apparently depicts God behaving badly, the proper approach will recognize that this tells us much more about human beings than about God.

I will end this description of the contextual approach to Scripture by citing two authoritative sources that support it. First, within the relatively conservative wing of modern Christian tradition, one author who is often accepted as thoughtful and dependable is C. S. Lewis. It is often assumed in these circles that Lewis was a biblical foundationalist, but this is mainly because he was careful to avoid too much theological drama in his popular work. But gifted as he was with both a penetrating mind and a deep love for the truth, he could not help but notice the biblical "texts of terror" and the theological problems these created. In particular, he recognized that if we link these dark texts too closely to divine agency by either accepting them as accurate images of God or by involving God too much in their production, we run the risk of finding a God who is evil and dangerous, and no longer worthy of our devotion. I would like for a few moments to consider in more detail Lewis's thoughts on this issue.

Lewis wrote a fairly popular book, *Reflections on the Psalms*, which takes up a position on the biblical psalms that curse our enemies. In this class of psalm, known among scholars as "imprecatory" psalms, he was confronted by an obvious theological question: How can we square a psalm that curses our enemy with the command of Jesus to love them? Given the popularity of the psalms among Christians, I suppose that many believers have asked the same question over the years.

As some of you may know, Lewis decided that the two viewpoints cannot be squared. Jesus was right, and the psalmists were wrong. Lewis said of the imprecations that "the human qualities of the raw materials show through. Naivety, error, contradiction, even (as in the cursing Psalms) wickedness are not removed" (Lewis 1958:111–12). Of course Lewis recognized these as human prayers and could say with a straight face that, in the psalms, what we're given are perfectly accurate depictions of humanity's highs and lows, including its sins. Fair enough. But what would Lewis do when the same sort of wickedness appeared in another genre, such as a narrative that depicts not only human beings but also God behaving poorly? Would he apply the same theological rationales to, say, the genocide in Joshua? Indeed, Lewis plainly tells us that this is what must be done. He writes:

Yes. On my view one must apply something of the same sort of explanation to, say, the atrocities (and treacheries) of Joshua. I see the grave danger we run by doing so; but the dangers of believing in a God whom we cannot but regard as evil, and then, in mere terrified flattery calling Him 'good' and worshiping Him, is a still greater danger. The ultimate question is whether the doctrine of the goodness of God or that of the inerrancy of Scriptures is to prevail when they conflict. I think the doctrine of the goodness of God is the more certain of the two. Indeed, only that doctrine renders this worship of Him obligatory or even permissible. (Beversluis 2007:295–96)

Lewis knows that the Israelites claimed divine sanction for the genocide, but he also knows that this cannot be right. I would guess that he regarded the book of Joshua as an Israelite attempt to baptize vice as virtue, though he doesn't say so. At any rate, if Lewis has it right . . . and I believe that he does . . . then our affirmation of the divine agency behind Scripture must leave room also for the finite, fallen human agents who shaped Holy Scripture. In this respect, the contextual approach tends to protect us from finding in Scripture a God who has been created in our own image.

Lewis enjoys only the authority of human reputation, so some of you will find his arguments compelling and others will not be impressed by them. But the second voice of support for the contextual view has this and more, in that he speaks to this question as a true authority in Christian theology. I refer here to Jesus Christ himself.

Within the text of his famous oration, the "Sermon on the Mount" (Matt 5–7), we find a series of cases in which Jesus takes up theological or ethical positions against the Pharisees and their legal colleagues. We will explore these "antithesis" statements in more detail later on in the lectures, but for my present purpose I require only one as an example. Jesus said to his audience:

You have heard that it was said, "An eye for an eye and a tooth for a tooth." But I say to you, Do not resist an evil-doer. But if anyone strikes you on the right cheek, turn the other also. (Matt 6:38–39)

In this case, like the others, Jesus cites one of the laws of Moses and then advances an alternative position.[12] It is difficult from our vantage point, as Christian supporters of Jesus, to imagine how this would have impacted his Jewish audience. No authority was greater in their eyes than the lawgiver, Moses, and no text had more authority than the law he delivered to them. That Jesus should cite the law and then suggest a better way could only mean that there was something wrong or missing with the biblical law as written.

Now later in the sermon, Jesus specifically says that he did not come "to abolish but to fulfill the law" (Matt 5:17). He is not throwing out the law of Moses. But it is clear in this case that the traditional *lex talionis*, when fulfilled, no longer pointed to the wisdom of retribution but rather to the wisdom of submission towards the aggressor. Jesus himself ultimately walked this path to Golgotha. While he provides no clear basis for this teaching in the immediate context, within the larger context of his sermon and mission it becomes clear that *love* provided the fundamental basis for his interpretation of the law (cf. Matt 5:43–46; 22:37–39). This approach to Scripture, which allows the biblical teachings of love to trump those that support violence, stands very close in spirit if not substance to the approach advocated in modern, contextual approaches to Scripture.

If we accept this contextualist line of thought, in part because Jesus himself appears to have followed it, then we still have a dangling theological thread to mend. We noted earlier, in our description of Foundationalism, that its advocates have cited numerous biblical texts that apparently support their belief in a perfect Bible. How should these be understood within the contextualist account of Scripture?

Because the contextual approach expects from the biblical authors something less than moral and ethical perfection, it is not troubled much by errors of less importance, such as in matters of history or in the conceptual aspects of anthropology or theology. So, even if some texts appear to support the foundational view of biblical perfection, the contextualist will admit in these cases that

---

12. This retaliation law appears in Exod 21:24; Lev 24:20; Deut 19:21.

the biblical authors may have thought more of their words than they ought to have thought. For example, if Paul meant what he said in 1 Thessalonians (2:13), that his words were "God's words" rather than "human words," then the contextualists will assume that Paul has overstated his case. For it is quite obvious that Paul wrote and spoke in the common language of his day and in some cases offered spurious theological arguments, such as his odd assertion that God's natural order dictates the proper hair-lengths for men and women (1 Cor 11:13–16). Paul's words were very human words, even if he did not realize it. In this case and a few others, it is possible that the biblical authors wrongly believed that they or someone else could write without error.

But generally, this is not what the contextualists think about these texts. More often they assume that foundationalists have made much more of them than the biblical authors intended. When Paul commended the Thessalonians (in the text just mentioned) for accepting his words as "God's words" rather than "human words" (1 Thess 2:13), he likely intended this as a metaphorical rather than literal claim. He knew good and well that the words he wrote were his own and not directly from God. Of course Paul claimed often in his letters to be speaking with divine authority, but just as often he implicitly and even explicitly acknowledged that he and his letters were less than perfect. In one of his letters to Corinth, for example, Paul admitted that he did not know, for certain, whether he had conducted his relationship with them in an appropriate way (1 Cor 4:4). In the same letter he distinguished between his own theological opinions, which make up most of the letter, from those he'd received "from the Lord" (presumably referring to the oral traditions from Jesus; see 1 Cor 7, esp. vv. 8–10). Paul argued that human beings see theology "through a glass darkly" (1 Cor 13:12)[13] and confessed his ignorance even respecting the very themes he wrote about (Rom 11:33–36). So again, the contextualist is able to accept Paul's authority without believing

---

13. Technically, Paul's words are "Now we see in a mirror unclearly" (*blepomen gar arti di' esoptou en ainigmati*), but given the quality of modern mirrors, his point is better captured with my paraphrase.

that Paul thought he could write errorless, perfect letters. Unlike Foundationalism, Contextualism does not assume that God's authority, when delegated to human beings, will ensure that these authorities speak and act with perfection.

Why do foundationalists and contextualists arrive at such different places when it comes to the Bible? When all is considered, I believe that the foundational and contextual viewpoints are different because they are differently disposed towards the truth and evidence. Despite the fact that centuries separated the author of Job from Jesus, and Jesus from Galileo, and Galileo from the modern world of C. S. Lewis, all of these persons were willing to question the religious *status quo* when the evidence pointed in new directions. Critical thinking is an essential element in spiritual thinking. But as Job and Jesus and Galileo (and not a few biblical scholars, such as Tyndale) have learned from experience, critical thinking not only leads us to the truth . . . but, sometimes, to persecution and death.

Summary:
Contextualism and Foundationalism

I have outlined in these lectures two basic approaches to Holy Scripture, the foundational view and the contextual view. Each advances a particular understanding of what makes Scripture "holy" and, on this basis, of its authoritative role for the Church.

In the foundational view, God sanctified the authors of Scripture to ensure that they produced a book that was completely divine and holy, entirely insulated from the foibles and errors of the human viewpoint. Whatever Moses or Ezekiel or Matthew or Paul wrote is precisely the same as what God has said to the Church and, as applicable, to the Jews before them. It follows that such a book, if read properly, will inevitably yield for the reader the unblemished word of God. Biblical authority equals divine authority. This is why Scripture should be construed as "Holy Scripture."

The contextual view lands in a different place. Based upon the combined evidence of biblical testimony and the phenomena of Scripture, it holds that God is in the habit of sanctifying and using broken human beings to achieve divine ends. Just as God chooses Christians today and sanctifies them to do the gospel work, so God has in the past selected and sanctified the biblical authors to compose the books of Scripture. It is in this sense that Scripture is "Holy Scripture." This approach to Scripture engenders a different understanding of biblical authority than is offered by the foundational approach.

Scripture's authority is derivative, not final. Just as a parent holds authority over a child and a government over its citizens, Scripture has authority not because it is perfect (for neither parents, nor governments, nor biblical authors are perfect) but because God, by divine authority, has co-opted the various canonical collections of Scripture (Protestant, Catholic, Orthodox, etc.) to serve the theological needs of God's people and, through them, the needs of the world. If we conflate God's authority over Scripture with the human viewpoints expressed in it, we have misunderstood the nature of Scripture and will inevitably misuse it.

The basic difference between the foundational and contextual approaches can thus be summarized like this: Foundationalism assumes that what the biblical authors said was precisely the same thing as what God has said and in some way is still saying, whereas Contextualism assumes that the biblical authors have provided partial and imperfect windows into what God has said and is saying.

In the end, we should admit that neither of these views of Scripture is wholly correct. Only God sees all things clearly, and all of us believe the "fake news" to some extent. But some perspectives are better than others, and I have suggested in this lecture, implicitly and sometimes directly, that the foundational view of Scripture is based on "fake news" about the Bible. God is certainly perfect, but the biblical authors were not and did not write a book that is perfect. The foundationalists, by embracing and protecting "fake news" reports of biblical perfection, have drifted into a system of theology that assumes the Bible is something that it is not. To give this up will not be easy for the foundationalist and will create an intuitive sense of loss. I know this from personal experience. But in the end, no harm is done—and perhaps much can be gained—when we lose what we in fact never actually had. In particular, I will argue that the advocates of biblical Foundationalism tend to follow in the wayward footsteps of Job's friends and the Pharisees.

The contextual approach has its own set of potential problems to consider. While it correctly understands that some texts and themes in Scripture depict theology more clearly and accurately than others, it can on this basis drift into a mode of theology that discounts the testimony of Scripture. My next lecture will address this theme, though I will admittedly attend more directly to the weaknesses in the foundational approach to Scripture.

Biblical Authority as Spiritual Bypass

"What should we do with these rejected, condemned, Jew-ish people? . . . Let us apply the ordinary wisdom of other nations like France, Spain, Bohemia . . . which expelled them from their country. For God's wrath is so great over them that through soft mercy they only become more wicked."

—MARTIN LUTHER[1]

L et us begin with points of agreement. Scripture was written to advance the spiritual health of humanity by connecting us with God through the person of Jesus Christ (John 5:39; Rom 15:4; 2 Tim 3:16–17). A further point of agreement is that our connection with God, when it is healthy, leads to a life of love for God and neighbor, including our enemies. These points of agreement are evidence that common theological ground is possible even when we disagree in fundamental ways on the nature of Scripture. In this, at least, we are fulfilling the prayer of Jesus that his followers would unite against the darkness in the world (John 17:20–23).

But the unity only goes so far. As most readers have already surmised, the two approaches to Scripture outlined in the previous lectures are roughly associated in our own day with two quite different brands of Christianity, which disagree not only about the nature of Scripture but also about loads of other theological and ethical issues. The boundaries dividing these groups are not clean

1. Translated and abridged from Luther 1543: 1989, 1994.

and neat. The foundationalists and contextualists often disagree among themselves, and it is common for some foundationalists to agree with some contextualists. Human diversity always outpaces our categories. But as a general pattern, the two sides do tend to embrace and value particular views of theology, ethics, social issues, and politics. While I and most readers are no doubt aware of all this, my goal has been and will continue to be that we steer as clear possible from these points of conflict and focus instead on the proverbial "principle of the thing." The key question to be discussed in this chapter is: How does our view of biblical authority relate to our spiritual health?

Flesh and Spirit

When the Bible depicts our religious condition in terms of "flesh" and "spirit" (see Rom 7–8), it refers to the conflict between our natural appetites and our desire and need for something more. Our human nature reflexively hates an enemy and celebrates their pain, but the spiritual person believes that greater satisfaction may be found if we care about and restore broken relationships with our foes. These conflicting impulses are not merely in opposition, as if the two sides are playing tug-of-war. Spirituality does not remove our natural appetites but rather controls and reshapes them, so that they're directed towards healthy rather than damaging means and ends.[2] Desires for safety, food, rest, justice, identity, relationships, intimacy, sex, play, and beauty can be pursued in ways that foster a better human condition but also, unfortunately, in ways that make our lives worse. C. S. Lewis expressed this about as well as anyone when he said, "Without the aid of trained emotions the intellect is powerless against the animal organism" (Lewis 2001:24).

---

2. For classical Christian expressions, see Augustine 1887:530; Aquinas 1981: 2.726 (= *Summa Theologica*, pt. I.II, q. 31, art. 7). These and more recent discussions (such as Adams 1999; Finnis 2011) are often based on a fairly rigid view of "natural law" that I would not accept, but the basic principle does not depend on a rigorous view of the natural order.

The conflict between flesh and spirit is visible at every level of human existence, from face-to-face interactions to international relations. Social patterns are visible in the conflict that we are wise to notice and understand. As Jesus himself pointed out, we find it very natural to exercise our best virtues within the context of our own family and social community (Luke 6:32–34). It is an inclination native to nearly every person in every culture. Much less natural, he says, is to turn our hearts towards those on the outside, towards our "enemies" and "sinners" (Luke 6:35). We are wired to love the people in our tribe and to fear and even hate those who are not (Wrangham 2019).[3] When it comes to insiders, we're expected to observe the "rule of law": to pursue fairness and equity amongst the people. But when it comes to outsiders, we easily slip into the "law of war," which, in the end, allows us to do whatever we must to take advantage of and defeat our foes.

Psychological research has documented that this "us against them" dynamic is not primarily a result of rational reflection but depends much more on our intuitions and feelings about how the world works (Haidt 2001; 2012; Beck 2011). When we perceive anyone or anything as lying outside the circle of what is good and proper, our emotional world protects us by generating feelings of distance. In much the same way that we're disgusted when we smell spoiled food, we become fearful, and disgusted, and perhaps even angry when threatened by human behaviors. While these responses are important and healthy when triggered by real threats, they are very much connected to our "flesh" and have not necessarily been ordered properly by the spirit. Job's friends were disgusted by Job, and the Pharisees by Jesus. From these cases, we learn that disgust and anger are triggered by how we believe the world is ordered and not necessarily by how it is actually ordered. We avoid the spiritual "leper" because he will perhaps infect us or others with his spiritual illness. But what if we, ourselves, have a log in our eye and are as

3. According to Wrangham (2019), human beings have a relatively low "reactive aggression" towards our immediate neighbors and a relatively high "proactive aggression" towards those we view as outsiders. We are, paradoxically, the nicest and also most violent species on the planet.

much or more leprous than our neighbor? And even if he is a leper, what would Jesus have us do? Was it not his habit to touch lepers, both those suffering with physical disease and those rejected by the religious people in Jewish society?

Disgust is considered (by most theorists) as one of our *basic* biological emotions, shared also with the primates, like chimps, who grimace at and reject spoiled food.[4] But it is only in humans, apparently, that this basic emotion becomes deeply attached to things like relationships and social identity and moral judgments. Researchers of this "disgust response" have measured both its extent and effects. Let us consider, as an example, the now famous study of newly married couples published by John Gottman and his colleague, Sybil Carrère (1999).

Gottman and Carrère wondered whether they could observe and document the feelings of spouses towards each other and, on this basis, predict whether the marriage would last or end in divorce. In order to ensure that they were measuring the emotional displays of the couples rather than more complex relational dynamics, they used only the first three minutes of data from each couple.[5] Gottman postulated that couples exhibiting high levels of mutual contempt and disgust would soon divorce, whereas those less disgusted, even if there was a lot of conflict, would not. During a six-year period after the initial observations and predictions, Gottman's team observed a very high correlation between their predictions and the outcomes. Marriages lasted when conflicts were set within a context that included a positive emotional basis, but they generally failed under the weight of instinctive contempt and disgust.

The main point, I suppose, is that we cannot love well when we are disgusted by "the other." And this is a serious problem if we care

4. The bibliography is immense. For introductory discussions, see Darwin 1896; Ekman 1973; Chevalier-Skolnikoff 1973; Ekman and Friesen 1975; Plutchik and Kellerman 1980; Ekman and Davidson 1994; Plutchik 2000; Preuschoft 2000; Parr, Waller, and Heintz 2008.

5. The couples were actually observed for longer than three minutes, but the first three minutes were used for one level of the study, with the results as described here.

much about love, for nothing is clearer in our experience than that we are sometimes or often disgusted with other people. We show contempt even for our family and friends, not to mention for those with different political preferences or with religious, ethnic, racial, sexual, and national backgrounds other than our own.

Unsettling but common in human experience is that group conflicts like these arise very organically and naturally, as if appearing out of thin air. In recent years, in places like Rwanda, and Bosnia, and Uganda, we've watched former neighbors turn on their friends and slaughter them like animals (Espeland 2007). We should not allow the relative peace and safety of our own situation (if that is the case) to blind us from these kinds of historical possibilities. The Christians in these countries, and those involved in the atrocities of Nazi Germany, apparently thought far too much of their spiritual condition.

Our visceral disgust towards "the other" has cognitive implications for our ethical and theological reasoning. I am not prepared to say at this point whether feelings or thoughts come first in our cycle of perception. I suspect that the question cannot be answered any more than the proverbial "chicken and egg" question, but let's leave that to one side. What we can say is that research confirms a close relationship between our group identity and our ethical ideas. An old but important study by Tamarin (1973:185–90) found that most Jewish children naturally accepted the morality of Israel's genocide against Canaan but rejected genocide when neither the perpetrators nor the victims were Jewish. That the research subjects were children is important, for this indicates, about as well as a study can, that our *natural* morality is biased to support and protect our group identity. Modern research demonstrates that the moral reasoning of mature adults is no less affected by this group bias (Granitz and Ward 2001; An, Marks, and Trafimow 2016; Moncrieff and Lienard 2018). Let us note, as a matter of interest, that the biblical authors condemned Pharaoh's genocide against Israel but celebrated Israel's conquest of Canaan.

It is at this point that something should be said about the natural effect of power and authority differentials on human social modalities. In a very famous experiment conducted at Stanford University in 1971, researchers created a simulated prison in which randomly selected male subjects acted as the prisoners and guards. No particular training was provided apart from these role assignments. What happened? In the words of the researchers:

> This simulated prison developed into a psychologically compelling prison environment. As such, it elicited unexpectedly intense, realistic and often pathological reactions from many of the participants. The prisoners experienced a loss of personal identity and the arbitrary control of their behavior which resulted in a syndrome of passivity, dependency, depression and helplessness. In contrast, the guards (with rare exceptions) experienced a marked gain in social power, status and group identification which made role-playing rewarding. (Haney, Banks, and Zimbardo 1973:69)

This study is pregnant with implications, but the most obvious is that human beings with power tend to quickly become oppressive towards and traumatize those under their authority. We'll not be surprised that the guards enjoyed their fantasies of power, but that the volunteer prisoners persisted in the study, even after it became truly oppressive, illustrates the degree to which oppressed people fall into a state of learned helplessness. The same dynamic arises very naturally in other scenarios where power differentials exist between groups, especially when these groups are defined in terms of racial, ethnic, gender, sexual, national, and economic differences. As the experiment illustrates, in *any* we/they scenario, the side with power will tend to exercise and preserve their comparative advantages, and this will inevitably cause biologically and socially triggered conflicts. Christian theology traditionally holds that human beings are fallen and broken beings. This is very true.[6]

While these general comments about "flesh and spirit" apply to humanity as a whole, the specific dynamic of spirituality plays

6. We also learned from the Stanford Prison Experiment that some research experiments are unethical in their effects on the human subjects. The result was a new research compliance modality, generally known as the "Institutional Review Board" or some permutation thereof.

out differently in each person. Our individual stories are profoundly unique. Each was born to a certain family and social context,
learned a certain language or languages, was taught to think in certain ways about what is true and false, or about what is appropriate
and inappropriate, and passed through a particular set of experiences, both good and difficult. Our views of religion and morality
were formed in this process and we bring these into all that we do.
Many of these views are healthy and virtuous, else neither we nor
our society would hold together as we do. But there is much in us
and in our world that is also broken and in need of healing. Preju-
dicial assumptions cause us to love and accept some people and to
hate and reject others, often with feelings of deep resentment and
disgust. Some of us are so wounded and broken that we cannot get
along even with those close to us, perhaps to the point that we feel
utterly alone in the world. Try as we may, none of us fully control
and rise above these base and damaging instincts.

What I have just said about human beings was as true of the
biblical authors as it is of us. This became evident in our last lecture, which documented not only the very good things in Scripture
but also the obvious limitations and vices of its human authors and
audience. In spite of God's role in the composition and canoniza-
tion of Scripture, these vices extended about as far as they could in
the wrong direction. Some of the authors advocated for what we
would normally call "genocide" and others for owning and beating of slaves. This reflects the disgust pattern described just above,
with the Canaanites filling the role of outsider in relation to Israel
and slaves in relation to its wealthy upper classes. Paradoxically
(but inevitably), the biblical authors not only reported the sin of
humanity but also acted as sinners in the process. Paul may have
been "foremost among sinners" (1 Tim 1:15), but he was by no
means the only one. These observations have profound implications for our approach to Holy Scripture.

Biblical Authority and Spiritual Bypass in Foundationalism

Foundationalists assume that the Bible speaks the truth on every page of every book. In some respects this is a good thing, insofar as it stems from their respect for divine authority and serious commitment to the canonical word. God is pleased when his people believe things because they believe in him. But if my earlier descriptions of the Bible are correct (and I believe they certainly are), then the Bible is not the perfect book the foundationalists take it to be. As I will now explain, this false belief can have very negative effects on our interpretation of Scripture, theological reflection, understanding of the larger world, and moral choices and behaviors. To anticipate the results, I will suggest below that biblical Foundationalism, as a system of thought, tends to follow a psychological pattern that John Welwood (1984) has famously called "spiritual bypass." It constructs arguments and rationales that are ostensibly "biblical" and "spiritual" in order to justify unhealthy behaviors.[7]

False Virtues

Let us begin with the great sixteenth-century Reformer, Martin Luther (1483–1546). He was a biblical foundationalist who came to Scripture, as we all do, with a mixed bag of virtues and vices. He turned to the Bible, or so it seemed, in order to more clearly understand and pursue what is virtuous and to uncover and eradicate his vices. This engagement was important because, as we have seen, many vices come to us so naturally that we're prone to believe they are virtues. Among other things, Luther learned from the Bible that when we are wronged, we must overcome our natural inclinations for revenge and return good for evil, leaving the righting of wrong to God. In his own words: "For a Christian is a man who knows no hatred or animosity at all against anyone, has no anger or revenge in

---

7. For much earlier philosophical critiques of this phenomenon, see Nietzsche 1887.

his heart, but simply love, mildness and beneficence" (Luther 1892: 210; cf. Matt 5:44; Rom 12:19; Deut 32:35).

While this approach to Scripture sounds and in principle is quite admirable, our Reformer friend brought to his reading of Scripture the aforementioned assumption that Scripture advances only messages of virtue and none of vice. And herein lies the basic problem for Foundationalism. Because the biblical authors were fully human and exhibit in their writings both error and vice, it can come about that Luther finds not only his virtues but also his natural flaws either modeled by or supported by the biblical authors. And because of this, he embraces even tighter the very defect that most needs to be healed. No matter how much the Bible teaches about love and grace towards his enemies, Luther can find plenty of room left in biblical theology for a "reap what they sow" outcome. Opportunities abound in this system of theology to baptize our vice as virtue.

We see the effect of this problem in Luther's sermon (in 1530) on the biblical command to "love your enemies" (Matt 5:44). Immediately after admitting that "a Christian is a man who knows no hatred," Luther provides a list of biblical texts in which the heroes of Scripture pronounced curses upon their enemies. As we will see, this was an open door for Luther's nearly unbridled animosity. In an ingenious twist of theology, Luther reasoned that the Christian must always show love towards his enemies, but that this same Christian, if entrusted as a minister of the gospel, is not only free but duty-bound to speak vile and hateful things against the enemies of God (Luther 1892:43, 211–12). As Luther expressed it: "to hate one's enemy . . . belongs to an office of divine appointment" (Luther 1892:215). In this way, Luther blended together two contrary streams of theology, one that called him to love his enemies and another that called him to hate them and wish them ill.

As a rule, Luther could do little more than attack his enemies with words. He hated the Catholic authorities and said so again and again, but the Pope was in Rome and the bishops enjoyed layers of political, religious, and geographical protection. What would Luther do if these limitations were removed, if he were free not only to speak ill of his enemies but also to recommend action against them? We find out in a short work he penned in 1543, "On the Jews and Their Lies."[8]

Towards the end of his life, about fourteen years after he wrote the great hymn, A Mighty Fortress, Luther became increasingly frustrated with the Jewish community in Germany. His response was a short but terrifying pamphlet that would turn most stomachs. I take no pleasure in reporting this but believe there is much to be learned from Luther's errors.

Luther described the Jewish community as "a Devil's nest" and suggested their systematic persecution by civil authorities. Among other things, he recommended that (1) all contact with Jews should be avoided and perhaps that their houses and schools should be burned down, (2) that the Jews should not be allowed to own homes but rather moved into stables, (3) that their religious literature should be confiscated, (4) that Rabbis should be forbidden under threat of death from teaching the Jews, (5) that the Jews should be excluded from travel within the country, (6) that their money and lands should be taken away from them, and (7) that all else failing, the Jews should be enslaved or ejected from the country. Luther described these as acts of "prayer and godliness," whose purpose was to rescue a few Jews "from the flame and violent heat."

Luther supported his cause, where he could, by citing Scripture. At a critical point in the argument he appealed to the laws of Deuteronomy, which commanded that God's people should destroy the natives of Canaan because of their false religion (Deut 7; cf. Deut 29:18–21). This biblical text provided the basis for his plan to destroy the schools and houses of the Jews and, by implication, for just about anything else he wanted done to them. Luther knew the Bible well, of course, and seems to have understood that Christians were required to show mercy (Barmherzigkeit) towards the Jews. But he argued that the usual "soft mercy" (sanfte Barmherzigkeit) of love would not work on the evil-hearted Jews. They

8. For a more accessible German version, see Luther 1880–1910:20.1860–2029. For an English translation, see Luther 1971:47.137–306.

would only respond to the gospel, if at all, when persecuted in acts of "severe mercy" (*scharfe Barmherzigkeit*).

From a religious and psychological standpoint, it is not easy to account for the dark turns in Luther's theology. Detailed discussions appear in many books and articles, including the recent and excellent discussions by Gritsch (2012) and Cary (2019:207–38). But whatever questions we may have about Luther, we should not imagine him as a dramatic exception to the rule. Many Christians before him and after him, even to this day, have quoted the Bible to justify the worst sorts of evil. Nineteenth-century justifications of slavery in the southern United States readily come to mind (Elliott 1860; Haynes 2002). But Luther's case was unique in the sense that he was a giant in Church history and that his words carried so much authority within the Church in Germany. His anti-Semitic pamphlet inspired the persecution of Jews for several centuries in Germany, reaching its horrible pinnacle in the Holocaust.

The National Socialists of the 1930s and early 1940s (the Nazis) loved Luther and constantly quoted his work in their propaganda (Probst 2012), for it was a key element in their strategy to conflate their political project with the emotive power of faith (Steigmann-Gall 2003). We must not forget certain lessons from this history, in that millions of German Christians not only supported the evil regime but actually voted it into power. Apart from this support in the elections, it is hard to see how Hitler and his party would have succeeded as they did. Shirer noted some decades ago, in his famous work, *The Rise and Fall of the Third Reich*, that is it difficult to understand the complicity of the German Christians in this debacle apart from the impact of Luther's influence (Shirer 1960:209).

I will not review here the theological drama of the years leading up to and during the Nazi era, in which a majority of Protestants and Catholics alike eventually fell into line with Hitler. For this the reader can consult several studies in my bibliography. But we should note with care that Hitler appealed to these Christians by promising to make a very weak Germany great again, and for this hope they willingly believed his "fake news" and compromised Christian principle until it was too late. As Martin Niemöller famously said:[9]

> First they came for the Communists
> And I did not speak out
> Because I was not a Communist
>
> Then they came for the Socialists
> And I did not speak out
> Because I was not a Socialist
>
> Then they came for the trade unionists
> And I did not speak out
> Because I was not a trade unionist
>
> Then they came for the Jews
> And I did not speak out
> Because I was not a Jew
>
> Then they came for me
> And there was no one left
> To speak out for me

Rank and file Protestants during the Nazi era were not "Bible thumpers" but were indeed biblical Foundationalists, committed fully to the authority of Scripture and the confessions of the faith. But like Luther and to an extent because of him, they found enough biblical support for Hitler's project to satisfy their religious sense of things. This is because, as we have seen, the Bible contains messages of unimaginable beauty but also of ethical darkness.

This brings us back to my initial point about the potential spiritual dangers of Foundationalism. Like anyone else, the Foundationalist will prefer those biblical texts that most appeal to his innate sense of theology and morality. But because he assumes these texts are both utterly clear and completely error free, he naturally assumes that his human interpretation of the Bible is

9. This is a popular poetic version of Niemöller's speech, delivered after the war in Frankfurt, Germany on 6 January 1946.

nothing other than the perfect word from God on high. And this perfect word easily becomes the lens through which our confused friend interprets the rest of Scripture. The biblical command to love our enemies is thus read in light of commands to kill them. If one reads Luther's pamphlet, *On the Jews and Their Lies*, one is struck by the utter arrogance of the result, that he could declare with an unflappable confidence that he stood with God and against the evil and darkness in the world. He unwittingly became a contributor to the worst kind of darkness. In essence, Luther replaced God's authority with his own voice, and this was possible because his view of Scripture virtually ensured that Scripture could only say what Luther wanted to find in it; and still, he thought it was the voice of God.

I trust that the significance of my lecture title, "Biblical Authority as Spiritual Bypass," is now becoming clear. The foundationalist view of biblical authority allows its advocates to unconsciously substitute their limited and broken interpretations of a limited and broken Bible for the final and perfect word of God. By this the foundationalist falls into the age-old temptation to put the self in God's place. In an act of "spiritual bypass," the foundationalist paradoxically uses spiritual and religious tools to avoid dealing with his spiritual darkness and blindness. In this scenario, the combined resources of Scripture, prayer, devotional readings, and fellowship with like-minded believers can create a false impression that we are in a healthy place when we are not. Perhaps our condition is not as dire as Luther's or the countless German Christians that eventually followed him, but the lessons of history should at least warn us that we're probably less healthy than we think and perhaps more susceptible to extreme error than we realize.

In the end, the Bible will not save us from vice if we wrongly assume that its human authors had and expressed no vices. With God's help and under God's authority, we must make good judgments about which biblical texts carry the most weight in our theology and which carry the least. But this is only a part of our theological solution because the Bible, while an important source of insight, is not the only source that God has provided to humanity.

False Vices

If biblical Foundationalism tends to reinforce our vices as false virtues, the opposite is also true. Let us consider *empathy*, for example. By empathy, I refer to our natural capacity to see the world through the eyes of another. When we are empathetic, we feel joy when we notice and understand our neighbor's good spirit, and sadness and pain when we appreciate their plight and suffering. This capacity is a fundamental element in our capacity for love.

Because parts of Scripture were written in periods and places where human oppression was accepted, it can come about that we find ourselves caught between this natural sense of compassion and the direct but misguided witness of Scripture's human authors. Consider, for example, these comments by John Henry Hopkins (1864:6–7) about nineteenth-century slavery in the United States:

> If it were a matter to be determined by personal sympathies, tastes, or feelings, I should be as ready as any man to condemn the institution of slavery, for all my prejudices of education, habit, and social position stand entirely opposed to it. But as a Christian . . . I am compelled to submit my weak and erring intellect to the authority of the Almighty. For then only can I be safe in my conclusions.

Here and in the rest of his book, one can sense the dispassionate tone of Hopkins. Although naturally moved, he admits, by the plight of the slaves, Hopkins finds it necessary to park this empathy on the proverbial curb so that he can attend to and follow the explicit directions of Scripture. This, he says, is the only safe bet a Christian can make. In the end, Hopkins elected to side with the Bible and the slave traders and against the abolitionists.

While it is true that our natural empathies guarantee neither good theology nor Christian morality, it is equally true, as we have just seen, that they are sometimes better guides to spiritual health than any particular text or lists of texts in Holy Scripture. When we wrongly assume as Hopkins did that the biblical text is always correct, we will be forced in cases, perhaps many cases, to numb our capacity for love out of a misguided allegiance to Scripture. Empathy is thus regarded as an impediment rather than pathway to our love for others. Virtue becomes vice.

Saint Augustine was wise and right, in my opinion, when he wrote that "Whoever, then, thinks that he understands the Holy Scriptures, or any part of them, but puts such an interpretation upon them as does not tend to build up this twofold love of God and our neighbor, does not yet understand them as he ought" (Augustine 1887b:533). So great was Augustine's commitment to this principle that he argued, just after this, that Christians grounded firmly in the habits of "faith, hope, and love" have no need for Scripture except to teach others (Augustine 1887b:534). While I don't agree with this last point, for I doubt that anyone can achieve this exalted spiritual condition, there is obviously some truth in his point. For during the early centuries of the Christian faith, as it spread out across the landscapes of Asia, Africa, and Europe, the first Christians pursued their relationships with God and each other with nary a Bible in hand.

At any rate, to return to our main theme: When we approach the Bible as if it is nothing other than the ultimate and final word of God on all subjects, vice can become virtue, and virtue can become vice. To be sure, this means we've misunderstood the human condition. But we've also, inevitably, misunderstood God.

False Understandings of the World

I mentioned in an earlier lecture that the Church has struggled to manage new scientific insights, in part because these often come up against biblical descriptions of the world that are based on ancient viewpoints. It was difficult, for example, for Christians to accept modern explanations of astronomy when the Bible seemed to describe an immovable earth (perhaps even a flat earth) at the very center of the cosmos. If my description of the Bible is accurate, then this problem is endemic to biblical Foundationalism. Because it assumes the ancient and mistaken viewpoints of the Bible are perfectly and scientifically accurate, it spends considerable energy trying to harmonize these with modern viewpoints or to discredit modern science altogether.

A modern parallel to the old debate about astronomy appears in current controversies about the evolutionary origins of humanity (Numbers 2006). Although the scientific evidence for biological evolution is even clearer now than the astronomical evidence was in the days of Copernicus and Galileo (see Boyd and Silk 2009; Ayala 2010), biblical foundationalists have written hundreds of books and created whole industries, including massive museums,[10] to support a set of alternative scientific facts. One is told in these sources that the earth is only a few thousand years old, that a world-wide flood is supported by geological evidence, that dinosaurs and humans once shared the earth, and that the fossil evidence is a hoax.[11] Contrary claims from evolutionary science are passed off as a pack of lies, generated (at best) by confused scientists or (at worst) by human beings bent on challenging the authority of God and Scripture. My primary point is that the biblical Foundationalists are susceptible not only to "fake news" about the Bible but also, consequently, to "fake news" about modern science.

One can argue, I suppose that little harm comes from believing false facts about science and the other disciplines of human knowledge. But the ultimate harm is perhaps worse than it might seem. Saint Augustine, in his treatise on Christian scholarship, defended at length our proper and profitable uses of secular knowledge (Augustine 1887b:544–45, 548–55). It was he who first argued forcefully that "all truth is God's truth," no matter who notices it.[12] As Augustine saw it, the Christian who eschews these sources of insight will be poorer in their understanding of Scripture and will, perhaps, embarrass the cause of Christ through ignorance.

10. https://creationmuseum.org/; https://arkencounter.com/.

11. https://www.creationscience.com/; https://answersingenesis.org/; https://www.icr.org/.

12. This is a paraphrase of "Let every good and true Christian understand that wherever truth may be found, it belongs to the Master" (Augustine 1887:545).

Much that we are learning these days about human beings is informed by an evolutionary understanding of our origins. When we ask why groups of people commit genocide (and why you and I hate our neighbor), it turns out that much of this is driven by biological tendencies to fear "the other" and to protect ourselves with violent emotions and means. Like most animals, we are instinctively aggressive when threatened, even if we don't know precisely the nature of the threat or its source (Ulrich et al. 1966; Schwartz 1989). And like most social animals, we instinctively react *en masse*, like bees, against groups that we don't trust (Haidt 2012:221–45). These are primitive emotional responses that we inherited from our pre-human ancestors. Sometimes they serve us well, but often they run counter to the more advanced responses necessary for healthy human societies and, ultimately, for spiritual health. We earlier discussed the perennial Christian struggle between "flesh" and "spirit." This is an ancient way of describing the struggle between the animal and human sides of our personalities. The more we understand this biological reality, the better our strategies for spiritual formation.

When we consider humanity's violent instincts, our minds turn naturally to certain kinds of behaviors, such as war and criminality and other abusive behaviors. Human beings across the spectrum tend to agree that these are social pathologies that we would gladly do without. But I want to consider here a particular expression of human violence that is very much debated, in that it is generally embraced as good and healthy by biblical Foundationalists but rejected as a social ill by many modern researchers. This debate provides a good example of the problem created when our approach to Scripture skews and distorts our understanding of the world in which we live.

Our theme is the corporal punishment of children. Scripture teaches clearly and often that children should obey and respect their parents, and that parents should pursue this end by violent means when necessary. The popular expression of this principle, "Spare the rod, spoil the child," is a rough paraphrase of Prov 13:24a. This and a list of related biblical texts are cited immediately below.

> On the lips of one who has understanding wisdom is found,
>> but a rod is for the back of one who lacks sense. (Prov 10:13)

> Those who spare the rod hate their children,
>> but those who love them are diligent to discipline them. (Prov 13:24)

> Discipline your children while there is hope;
>> do not set your heart on their destruction. (Prov 19:18)

> Condemnation is ready for scoffers,
>> and flogging for the backs of fools. (Prov 19:29)

> Blows that wound cleanse away evil;
>> beatings make clean the innermost parts. (Prov 20:30)

> Folly is bound up in the heart of a boy,
>> but the rod of discipline drives it far away. (Prov 22:15)

> Do not withhold discipline from your children;
>> if you beat them with a rod, they will not die.

> If you beat them with the rod,
>> you will save their lives from Sheol. (Prov 23:13–14)

> A whip for the horse, a bridle for the donkey,
>> and a rod for the back of fools. (Prov 26:3)

> The rod and reproof give wisdom;
>> but a mother is disgraced by a neglected child. (Prov 29:15)

That this theme was taken seriously in ancient Israel is reflected in its repetition and in the consequences it allayed, such as an early death in Sheol (Prov 23:14b) or the possibility of capital punishment (Deut 21:18–21). The authors of Proverbs believed that human success depended on the formative influence of physical discipline.

Some biblical texts, particularly in the New Testament, seem to point in a somewhat different direction. Parents are instructed on several occasions to avoid provoking their children to anger (Eph 6:4; Col 3:21), which can be understood as placing some kind of practical limit on the extent of physical punishment. Some foundationalists, such as Wenger (2005:725–26), have argued on this basis that Proverbs itself forbids parents from causing harm. While we could all wish this were true, it is fairly clear that Proverbs compares this discipline to the beating of animals and allowed even for the physical wounding of children (as was also the case in ancient Israel for slaves).[13] In other words, some biblical authors apparently permitted more violent parenting than others. Jesus also had some things to say about children, which I will discuss a bit later.

As the reader undoubtedly knows and perhaps has experienced, biblical Foundationalists have generally accepted and followed these directives from antiquity up to the present day (see the survey in Greven 1990). What does contemporary research have to say about these Scriptural teachings and to parents who accept and apply them in the education of children?

Amongst both humans and our animal relatives, physical aggression is a natural response to a perceived threat. It is the "fight" option within a "fight, flight, or freeze" routine that's hard-coded in our biology (Goldstein 2010). Now within human beings, aggression takes on an additional role, for it arises not only as a triggered reflex but also as a calculated behavior. It is, for example, a tried and tested strategy for exerting control over other people. The powerful often use force and threats of force to coerce behaviors amongst the powerless. Although our biological systems have evolved to support advanced cooperative behaviors and we've developed cultural traditions, such as law and religion, to shape and curb our violent impulses, these "safeguards" have not prevented some very dark stretches of human history (Wilson 1975; 1978). But on the whole, human beings tend to get along well enough to create stable societies and cultures.

The biological and social history that has brought us to this point is as fascinating as it is difficult to explain, but it is obvious (in my opinion) that in actual practice we've gradually managed

13. See Prov 20:30; 26:3; Deut 21:18–21; Exod 21:20–21.

in some cases to become less violent than our forebears (Pinker 2011; Wrangham 2019). Slavery, racism, sexism, domestic violence, and other social ills have been confronted with significant, if insufficient, progress in our own country and many others. If one steps back and looks across the waterfront of human rights, the real surprise is that children remain the only group that can be legally and routinely hit by adults whenever an adult wishes to do so. Within the United States, a majority of parents with toddlers routinely strike them (Straus 2001:165; Smith et al. 2013:427).

There was a time when it made sense to believe that hitting children served them well, but lots of research has demonstrated that this is entirely false. Psychologists, sociologists, and criminologists report that even modest uses of corporal punishment have negative impacts on children and on their relationships with parents and others. Statistically speaking, these children have weaker attachments to parents than other children; they are more angry, depressed, suicidal, violent, and masochistic; they have lower self-confidence, poorer academic outcomes, and are less obedient to social rules and norms; and they also show less creative initiative and are more likely, as adults, to become alcoholics and physically abusive (Straus 2001; Marshall 2002; Gershoff and Grogan-Kaylor 2016). In sum, aggressive parenting does not form children into loving, happy people but rather into aggressive, depressed people. This assessment rests on strong evidence from cross-sectional correlations, longitudinal data, and meta-analytical studies.

Most Christian parents in the United States believe, nevertheless, that corporal punishment is an effective tool for training children. That this is the case makes some sense, for hitting children certainly provides an immediate control over their behavior and is presented in the Bible as the gold standard for teaching and training in spiritual righteousness. But in the end, this strategy is actually based on "fake news" about Scripture and about the actual, documented effects of corporal punishment.

Biblical foundationalists imagine that the Bible, when it recommends hitting children, is offering a fresh and novel approach to parenting. It is not. The ancient authors of Scripture were merely following the standard wisdom of their day, which was understood for generations as the best and most natural way to ensure that children did not disrupt the proper order of family and society. Their views were not informed by modern psychological and sociological research any more than the author of Genesis was informed by the modern insights of astronomy and geology.

As I have said, we have gradually learned in our own country and many others to better honor the image-bearing dignity and value of human persons. Physical violence against our neighbor has at this point been outlawed against nearly every class of person, with the exception of children. Why is this the case? To put it simply: children are still suffering physical punishments because they have no power, no voice, and are essentially defenseless. This has made it very easy to perpetuate violence against them under the aegis of divine authority and parental wisdom. But the practice of hitting children, while just as biblical as hitting slaves, is no healthier nor appropriate if our goal is to honor the humanity of each person. This is *obvious*.

Biblical foundationalists will either be unaware of all of this research on corporal punishment or will appeal to a parallel research library with its alternative facts and conclusions. While those interested in the theology of corporal punishment should certainly read and consider these foundationalist resources, it is important, in my opinion, to realize that they are grounded in the same assumptions that provided the "alternative facts" of sixteenth-century Christian astronomy and the "alternative facts" of modern Christian biology. In spite of what some biblical texts say, these things remain true: the earth goes around the sun, humans evolved from earlier life forms, and hitting children is a bad idea. Anything else is "fake news" based on false facts.

It is at this point that I'll add to our discussion something from the teachings of Jesus about children. While some Christian theologies paint their spiritual condition in dark shades and on this basis justify corporal punishment—our friend Augustine is a good example (1887a:48)—one does not find anything like this expressed during the savior's ministry. On the contrary, Jesus taught his adult audience that they must become like children if they hoped to enter eternal life (Matt 18:1–5; cf. von Balthasar 1991). Rather than accentuate the sinfulness of children and their potential to outgrow it through spiritual training and nurture, as Augustine does, Jesus implied that a greater problem is that children learn how to sin from adults (Matt 18:6–7). Of course, he was making one and not many points with these comments. Certainly he realized that children need to grow up spiritually and, though he does not speak to this, that they inherit in their person the broken conditions of the world. But Jesus did not see, to find spiritual guilt in children, nor did he foist upon them the spiritual darkness that many theologies, especially Protestant theologies, often do. One finds within the Eastern Orthodox traditions a spiritual view of children, sick but guiltless, that is closer to the views of Jesus (Ware 1992:218–25). Jesus does not tell us what he thought about the corporal punishment of children, but his perspective on children better suits the insights of modern psychological and social research than do the teachings offered in the book of Proverbs. Rather than drive the folly out of our children, we'd be wiser to observe and learn from their humility. This is, at least, how Jesus saw it.

Further Spiritual Impacts of Biblical Foundationalism

While the imprisonment of Galileo, the Nazi debacle, Southern slavery, violence towards children, and countless other dark turns and features in human history should not be blamed entirely on biblical Foundationalism, there is no doubt that it shoulders a part of the blame. The followers of Jesus should have stood firmly against rather than supported these oppressive forces, but too often our view of the Bible prevented or severely limited our capacity to shine light into the darkness. An important cause of this limitation has been two false assumptions about the Bible—first, that it includes no errant human viewpoints, and second, that biblical insights are necessarily superior, in all cases, to the extra-biblical insights of human observation and research.

Two negative spiritual effects can be anticipated if this is the state of affairs, one upon the Christian and another upon those who are not Christians. The first effect is laid out by Augustine in *On Christian Doctrine*, when he contemplates the possible effect of the Bible's contradictions on the spiritual health of the Christian:

> For if he [the reader of Scripture] takes up rashly a meaning which the author whom he is reading did not intend, he often falls in with other statements which he cannot harmonize with this meaning. And if he admits that these statements are true and certain, then it follows that the meaning he had put upon the former passage cannot be the true one: and so it comes to pass, one can hardly tell how, that . . . he begins to feel more angry with Scripture than he is with himself. And if he should once permit that evil to creep in, it will utterly destroy him . . . Now faith will totter if the authority of Scripture begins to shake. And then, if faith totters, love itself will grow cold. (Augustine 1887b:533)

Augustine was a biblical foundationalist and I am not, but we agree that the reader of Scripture will find apparent contradictions in it and that, if they hold fast to them, the result is theological frustration and perhaps the loss of love for God and neighbor. In the spirit of his Foundationalism, Augustine recommended that the reader use allegories in these cases, especially when the conflict is of a moral nature and could imply that God or the characters or authors of Scripture are behaving badly (Augustine 1887b:533, 560–62). While I would prefer this approach over those that are inevitably stuck with all of the Bible's natural meanings, the better solution (I have argued) is to use a contextual approach in our interpretation of Scripture. Apart from these solutions, the Christian foundationalist, particularly one thoughtful and inquisitive, is forced again and again to fit together contrary biblical texts and to manage an ever-expanding list of conflicts between Scripture and public knowledge. As the reader probably knows, innumerable defections from the faith have resulted from this confusing and often gut-wrenching experience.

Needless to say, if the conflict between Scripture and public knowledge creates doubt for the Christian it is apt to create even greater barriers to faith among those who are not within the Church. How can one embrace the Christian faith if it is attached to misguided ideas about the Bible and, because of this, to false facts about science, psychology, sociology, history, and other things? The gospel in this situation looks like fake news. And the situation is even worse if, because of these errors, foundationalists align themselves with moral, ethical, and political positions that run up against the Christian priorities of love and compassion for the poor and oppressed. As Jesus said and the old song says, "They will know we are Christians by our love" (John 17:23). We will take up this important theme, Christian love, in the next lecture.

Spiritual Bypass in Contextualism

I have been fairly critical of biblical Foundationalism, for this has been and is the primary theme of my lectures. I have advanced as an alternative the contextual approach to Scripture, but even this, however better in certain ways, is not immune to the effects of fake news and spiritual bypass. Contextual approaches to the Bible are not encumbered by the illusion of biblical perfection nor, because of this, by an inherently insular view of the larger world and of the human condition. In principle this is an advantage over Foundationalism. But these freedoms are only healthy when they are deployed in the name of truth rather than license.

The right-wing Christians who most supported Hitler in his early days, an "Aryan" movement known as the *Deutsche Christen*, were biblical contextualists if they cared about Scripture at all.[14] Although they appealed to Scripture in some cases, the driving force in their thought was social and biological Darwinism

---

14. The term used here, *Deutsche Christen*, literally translates as "German Christians" but does not refer to the general population of German Christians but rather to this particular anti-Semitic, pro-Aryan religious group. As we have seen, a majority of the Christians in Germany eventually supported their agenda either explicitly or tacitly.

(Weikart 2013), from which they (ostensibly) inferred the superiority of their own Aryan race over the Jewish race and over other races and groups. So great was their hatred of the Jews that, after persecuting and killing them, they labored to eradicate from German society every remaining trace of their existence. The Bible, with so much Jewish content, represented an obvious challenge for this agenda, but the *Deutsche Christen* were not to be denied. They jettisoned the entire Hebrew Bible and, with a few historical sleights of hand, deftly turned Jesus into an Aryan hero (Steigmann-Gall 2003; Heschel 2008). This revisionist agenda was easy to pursue if one did not care about the truth of things, but in this case the *Deutsche Christen* found support for their agenda in the insights of modern biblical criticism (Steigmann-Gall 2003:8, 33). This approach to the Bible, which emerged in Germany and in Europe generally during the nineteenth century, held that the Bible, in terms of its nature and origins, was much more human than traditional theology had earlier supposed. The *Deutsche Christen* exploited this open door to criticize and revise anything and everything they did not like in Scripture.

By blending their faith with Nazi ideology, the *Deutsche Christen* participated in one of the most heinous acts of spiritual bypass in human history. When it comes to the Bible and religious faith, there are many ways to get things wrong. I will pick up this theme just below.

Summary and Conclusions

Biblical Foundationalism (as represented by Martin Luther) and Contextualism (as represented by the *Deutsche Christen*) erred in entirely different ways but for the same basic reason. In both cases, they construed theology in a way that made themselves rather than God the final authority in matters of faith and practice.

In Luther's foundational approach, the Bible was treated as a perfect book and Luther as a perfect interpreter. By this, Luther transformed whatever he found written in the Bible into nothing other than the perfect word of God. Hatred for his enemies became God's hatred because he found this agenda clearly expressed in the Bible. And this points us to the fundamental error of biblical Foundationalism. It replaces God's authority with the authority of the human author of Scripture and, ultimately, with the human interpreter of Scripture. As a result, our spiritual journey with God, and the necessary process of learning to listen to and follow God's voice, is truncated in all of the ways we've discussed in this lecture, and others besides.

As for the contextual approach of the pro-Ayran *Deutsche Christen*, their basic assumption about Scripture was the same as in all contextual approaches, namely, that the Bible is a diverse and complex document and advances many rather than one theological and historical perspective. We learn from this example that Contextualsim, even if it offers theoretical advantages over Foundationalism and hence, potentially, practical advantages, is not a sure-fire solution for biblical interpretation. No less than any approach to Scripture, the utility of Contextualism ultimately depends on whether the Christian reader of Scripture is committed to God as the final authority over Scripture or is leveraging the human diversity of Scripture, in an act of spiritual bypass, to serve unholy ends. The *Deutsche Christen* followed the second path.

Of course, the cases of Luther and the *Deutsche Christen* are extreme in comparison to whatever is going on these days amongst most biblical foundationalists and contextualists. Fine Christian people stand on both sides of the debate about biblical authority, and this proves that our theological beliefs about the Bible do not determine in any fixed way our particular spiritual and ethical destinations. But the examples of Luther and the *Deutsche Christen* should be taken seriously, nonetheless, else we're apt as human beings to sooner or later fall into the same traps. In the next chapter, we shall consider an approach to Scripture that accentuates the final authority of God in our theology and, hopefully, opens up for us a better trajectory than was followed by Luther and the *Deutsche Christen*. Each of these approaches to faith, in a different but distinctive way, ended in the dark cul-de-sac of hatred and anti-Semitism.

Reading Scripture under God's Authority

"He taught them as one having authority, and not as their scribes."

—MATT 7:29

Introduction

I noted in the first lecture that Scripture calls us, in the spirit of Job and Jesus, to pursue the theological truth of things no matter how inconvenient and unpopular the destination might be within our faith community. During the course of the second, third, and fourth lectures, I took up this duty with respect to the pressing question of the nature of Scripture and of its authority in light of that nature. Here I described two basic approaches to Scripture, the foundational and contextual approaches, and argued that Contextualism represents more faithfully the human character of God's written word. I noted that Foundationalism, though inferior on this point, is quite persistent within the Church because it is supported by "fake news" about the Bible, to the effect that each page of Scripture agrees not only with all of the others but also with every possible source of insight and knowledge available to human beings. I explained at length, in the previous lecture, that this construal of Scripture is mistaken and can have very negative impacts on biblical interpretation, human knowledge, spiritual formation, and the gospel witness of the Church. I admitted, however, that the Contextual approach, even if theoretically and potentially better, will not necessarily yield a better result. This is because a correct view of the nature of Scripture is a bit like the first number on a combination lock. Unless the other numbers are correct, the lock will not open. The question is: How should readers of Scripture properly open the lock to this sacred repository of divine wisdom?

Reading Scripture with Jesus Christ

As a biblical scholar, I am expected to respond to this question with a flurry of technical and theological insights. Appeals would be made to the Hebrew, Aramaic, and Greek languages, to the details of ancient history, to the cultural and religious backgrounds of the Near Eastern and Greco-Roman worlds, and to the modern disciplines that presumably make these sources more intelligible, such as sociology, anthropology, theology, and philosophical hermeneutics. While my approach in this lecture will not entirely disappoint the reader who is looking for this, my theme in what follows is rather narrow and will not yield any novel or holistic theory of biblical interpretation. Rather, my purpose in this lecture is to learn how to better read the Bible by observing how Jesus read it.[1]

I should make clear, from the outset, that I have no interest in portraying Jesus as a clairvoyant first-century representative of twenty-first-century biblical scholarship, as if he somehow operated with the same sources and resources, and the resulting insights, that provide some advantages for modern research. We hold that he was divine but also a man of his time, a Jew who "grew in wisdom and stature" (Luke 2:52), who knew not when the end would come (Mark 13:32), and who interpreted the Bible in relation to his own context and frame of reference. My point is not that Jesus was limited, although this is apparently true, but rather that this is an advantage for the modern Christian. By observing how Jesus related Scripture to his own concrete social context, we are able to better imitate and apply his habits in our own concrete situations.

---

1. As I stated in the first lecture, my discussion will not attend closely to the differences between the historical Jesus from the Jesus of tradition as described in the gospels.

For reasons that I hope will become clear, I would like to begin with the very famous "Good Samaritan" story in Luke 10.

The Good Samaritan
(Luke 10:25–37)

The Samaritan sect of ancient Judaism is fascinating. Because of its origins in the north of Israel, the sect was insulated from canonical developments within larger Judaism and accepted as Holy Scripture only the five written books of Moses and a version of the book of Joshua (Anderson and Giles 2005). They rejected the prophetic books, the books of the Writings, and the oral Torah of Judaism. Even what they accepted the Samaritans edited to taste, so that their version of the Pentateuch no longer pointed to Jerusalem but rather to Mt. Gerizim as the place where God should be worshipped. One obvious theological effect of these canonical moves was that the Samaritans, having rejected books like Ezekiel and especially Daniel, did not believe in the resurrection to a blissful afterlife.[2] Like the Sadducees, who also accepted only (or at least, primarily) the written books of Moses, Samaritan personal eschatology was simple: the soul is eternal, but when you're dead and in Sheol . . . you're dead and in Sheol. End of story.

It is fairly easy to see why traditional Jews viewed the Samaritans as heretics. To put this in their own words, the Jews wrote in *Maseket Kutim* 2:8: "When shall we take them [the Samaritans] back? When they renounce Mount Gerizim, and confess Jerusalem and the resurrection of the dead" (Montgomery 1907:203). I should note in passing that it is believed by some, on the basis of *Memar Marqe*, that a belief in the resurrection eventually emerged among some Samaritans by the fourth century AD, but Dexinger has pointed out that the *Marqe* manuscripts are in poor condition and probably do not refer to the resurrection at all (Dexinger 1989). All that we know about the Samaritans, explicitly from both Christian and Jewish sources and implicitly from the Sadduccean

2. Montgomery 1907:239–40; Coggins 1975:131–48; Origen 2009:154; Sifre Num. 112; b. Sanh. 90b.

analogy, indicates that around the turn of the era, they did not believe in the resurrection.

This brings us to my favorite biblical story, the tale of the Good Samaritan. "What must I do to inherit eternal life?," asked an educated lawyer. With prompting from Jesus, the lawyer quickly answered his own question: "we must love God . . . and we must love our neighbor." Jesus agreed. This is how one wins eternal life. For convenience we may refer to this, following Scot McKnight, as the "Jesus Creed" . . . so long as we remember, as implied by this very text, that Jesus may have inherited rather than invented the idea that Deut 6:5 and Lev 19:18 together summarize the Law's requirements.[3]

At any rate, the lawyer, apparently uncomfortable with the possible implications of his own solution, at once moved to exonerate himself with a simple question: "Who is my neighbor?" By this he meant: Should I follow Scripture strictly in Lev 19:18, which enjoins love only for my "brothers" (19:17) and "the sons of [my] people" (19:18), or should I extend this in principle to those not mentioned in the text? Jesus answered with a story.

As all of us know, a man, presumably Jewish, was robbed, beaten, and left for dead on the roadside between Jerusalem and Jericho. Two Jews well-versed in the law saw him but passed by on the other side of the road. Then a Samaritan saw him and, in a socially unexpected turn of events, was moved with compassion. The Samaritan dressed the victim's wounds, took his Jewish neighbor to an inn and cared for him, and left with the innkeeper both money and promises to safeguard the injured man's welfare. That Samaritans were often despised by the Jews further thickens the plot, since in this case the suffering Jew is saved by his "enemy" rather than by his "friends."

3. Of course the text of Luke itself, if historically accurate in the details, is direct evidence that this tradition was current within Judaism during the life of Jesus. Philo of Alexandria (c. 20 BC to AD 50) viewed love for God and neighbor as a summary of the Decalogue (see *de Decalogo* 50–51, 108–110, 121 [in Philo 1929–1953: vol. 7] and *Quis rerum* 168 [in Philo 1929–1953: vol. 4]). For a much later sixth century AD Jewish source, see Lev. Rab. 24:5. For other sources and discussion, see Roloff 2000:98–99.

Three travelers saw the ill-fated victim. What was the difference between them? Only one was moved by "compassion." Only one "loved his neighbor" in an act that erased the wall of animosity between the Jew and his Samaritan "enemy." Commentators often highlight the ethnic and theological irony intended by Jesus . . . ethnic, because a Samaritan bests by far the conduct of two orthodox Jews . . . theological, because the Jews will not jeopardize ritual practice for the sake of a fallen comrade (Lev 21:1–4; cf. Fitzmyer 1984:882–85). But the irony is deeper, verging on the sardonic. Namely, in this story we find that the Samaritan, who does not believe in eternal life, shall receive it because he loved his neighbor, while the two Jews—who do believe in eternal life—will miss out. In the theology of Jesus as depicted by Luke, love takes priority over doctrine. In fact, when it comes to eternal life, in this story it seems that love is the only thing that matters: "Do this, and you will live" (Luke 10:28).

In some respects, all of this is well known to the reader. The story is familiar, and the emphasis that Jesus places on love for God and neighbor has become standard jargon in Christian circles. One could wonder what's new here. For starters, the fact that a heretic could merit eternal life *merely* because he loved his neighbor well, quite apart from whether he even believed in the afterlife, certainly has some kind of implication for our traditional notions of soteriology. Our approaches to salvation often emphasize proper doctrine rather than emotional dispositions and actions. But the story's deeper value for theology, I believe, is that it confronts a natural but quite mistaken application of Jesus's teaching about love. The Jesus creed, that the whole of Scripture is summed up as love for God and neighbor, is easily "translated" to mean that love provides the proper *foundation* for our interpretation of Scripture. This is true so far as it goes but does not go far enough. For we learn from the Good Samaritan that love is not only the proper *foundation* for understanding and applying the Bible but also its proper *destination*.

The priests and Levites of the first century knew that love was a fundamental principle of Jewish piety. But because Scripture taught that they should not touch the dead or by implication those possibly dead (Lev 21:1–4), they reasoned that love, whatever it meant, was best served by adhering to God's written word and by preserving the purity of Judaism as prescribed in it. This sort of logic, which only begins but does not end with love as the goal, is what Jesus did not accept. The theology of the Samaritan was grounded in love as the outcome rather than first principle of life. This is why he loved better, and why he, rather than the orthodox Jews, merited eternal life.

The practical power of this story was documented a few decades ago by Wuthnow (1991:157–87), who found a high correlation between people who knew the story of the Good Samaritan and those engaged in charity and social-service activities. In contrast, if we're looking in this story for our old friends, the biblical Foundationalists, we find them in the priest and Levite.

Jesus and the Law in the Sermon on the Mount (Matt 5:21–48)

For a more direct application of this principle to the interpretation of Scripture, we can turn to the very famous sermon that Jesus preached on a mountainside in Galilee. The critical section of this sermon for biblical interpretation appears in the Matt 5, where he quotes and then comments on the law of Moses. Noteworthy is that Jesus introduces his comments with these words: "Don't assume that I came to destroy the Law or the Prophets. I did not come to destroy but to fulfill" (Matt 5:17). As commentators have often noted, Jesus anticipates here an objection that may arise in his audience from his approach to the law. While Jesus commits himself with these words to the law of God, and we as Christians believe him on this point, his actual interpretations look in some cases like outright contradictions of the law. After all, as we shall see just below, his commentaries are cast in terms of *antitheses* that advance novel alternatives to what is actually written in the law. This is an important point to which I will return below. The relevant quotations are as follows (with the legal references from the law in footnotes):

> You have heard that it was said to our ancestors, "Do not murder, and whoever murders will be subject to judgment."[4] But I tell you, everyone who is angry with his brother will be subject to judgment. (Matt 5:21–22)
>
> You have heard that it was said, "Do not commit adultery."[5] But I tell you, everyone who looks at a woman to lust for her has already committed adultery with her in his heart. (Matt 5:27–28)
>
> It was also said, "Whoever divorces his wife must give her a written notice of divorce."[6] But I tell you, everyone who divorces his wife, except in a case of sexual immorality, causes her to commit adultery. (Matt 5:31–32)
>
> Again, you have heard that it was said to our ancestors, "You must not break your oath, but you must keep your oaths to the Lord."[7] But I tell you, don't take an oath at all . . . But let your word 'yes' be 'yes,' and your 'no' be 'no.' (Matt 5:33–34, 37)
>
> You have heard that it was said, "An eye for an eye and a tooth for a tooth."[8] But I tell you, don't resist[s] an evildoer. On the contrary, if anyone slaps you on your right cheek, turn the other to him also. (Matt 5:38–39)
>
> You have heard that it was said, "Love your neighbor and hate your enemy."[9] But I tell you, love your enemies and pray for those who persecute you, so that you may be sons of your Father in heaven. (Matt 5:43–45)

---

4. Exod 20:13; Deutt 5:17; Gen 9:5.

5. Exod 20:13; Deut 5:17; Lev 20:10.

6. Deut 24:1.

7. Lev 19:12; Num 30:3; Deut 23:24.

8. Exod 21:24; Lev 24:20; Deut 19:21.

9. Lev 19:18; Deut 7:1–2; cf. Pss 5:5; 11:5; Prov 6:16.

Although these quotations and their meanings will perhaps seem straightforward to us, the legal issues and debates that lie behind them had long histories and were incredibly complex. When the Jews finally wrote down these interpretive traditions, which in the days of Jesus existed mostly in oral form, thousands of pages were the result.[10] In my opinion, the best and most accessible discussion of these legal issues as they relate to Matt 5 is by Neudecker (2014), to which I refer the reader for a more detailed discussion. A further difficulty is that Jesus was prone to use hyperbolic imagery, such as turning the other cheek, plucking out the eye, or cutting off the right hand in order to achieve spiritual health (Luz 2007:240; Evans 2012:124). We must therefore be careful about pushing the implications of his literal words too far.

Regardless, one readily notices a two-fold pattern in the biblical interpretations of Jesus. First, he is not satisfied with mere adherence to the letter of the law. He demands that his followers get to the moral root of each requirement, in this way assuming that the proper goal of spirituality is to become a different person rather than only to behave differently. Thus, Jesus extends the laws for adultery and murder so that the underlying thoughts that lead to them, lust and hatred, are themselves contrary to the intentions of Scripture. By the same logic, he rejects oath-taking because this will imply we are honest only under threat and not as a matter of habit. I take it that we are intuitively drawn to this kind of logic, even if we know, as readers, that the bar of spiritual health has been raised considerably.

Secondly, in some cases Jesus seems to interpret the law so differently that he appears to reverse it. Respecting divorce, for example, he no longer permits this for any and every reason, as does the law of Moses in Deuteronomy (24:1), but only in certain, limited cases. Some Jewish leaders noticed and were obviously troubled by this interpretation, as we'll see later on in the gospel of Matthew, in chapter 19. We will discuss that text and the debate it describes in the next section of the lecture.

10. For example, see the Mishnah in Danby 1933.

The sense of reversal is even stronger in two other cases, where Jesus challenges interpretations of law that permit violence in response to violence. In one of these, he rejects the logic of "eye for an eye" justice in favor of responses that, I suppose, could be described as acts of love, such as turning the other cheek or going the extra mile. In another, he by the same logic extends the law of love from friends only to the whole of humanity, including even our enemies. As we have noted already in our discussion of the Samaritan story, Jesus interprets these laws so that their concrete destination is an expression of love rather than apathy or violence.

The inquisitive reader will have a question at this point. Although Jesus claimed that his teachings did not reject but rather fulfilled the law, how can we square this claim with his actual readings of Scripture when these seem, in some cases, to flatly contradict the clear letter of the law? While this question is not easily answered, two observations are in order. As Neudecker (2014) points out in his study of this theme, the Jewish tradition was already leaning in the direction of Jesus on some of these points. The rabbinic sources show that "eye for an eye" retribution was understood already, in the days of Jesus, to be too extreme, and a reluctance to take oaths was likewise native to Jewish tradition. This "liberal" trend, which emphasized the spirit rather than letter of the law, was advanced by the rabbinic school of Hillel against the school of Shammai, which preferred a more literal approach (Telushkin 2010; cf. Sonne 1945). When Jesus took up positions that appear contrary to the written law, he was not alone; he was participating within and in relation to traditional Jewish debates about Scripture.

The reason for this trend is related to my second observation. In the debate between Hillel and Shammai, Hillel was the ultimate winner. The tendency within Judaism to embrace this more liberal approach stemmed, undoubtedly, from pragmatic necessity but also from the natural compassion of some Jewish scholars. Whether they realized it or not, their softer positions on the law were based on emotional and social concern rather than on rational arguments from the legal letter. While this represented real progress, Jesus (and some other Jews) apparently believed that natural compassion did not take them far enough.

When Jesus taught that neighborly love included even our enemies, this was a truly new and radical concept. No precedent for this position appears in any school of rabbinic Judaism; it does not appear even as a rejected viewpoint in the legal debates (Neudecker 2014:109–28). That this was the case is not a great surprise, since Jews had lived under oppressive regimes for centuries leading up to and during the life of Jesus. Only with difficulty will the oppressed, whether Jew or Gentile, feel love for the oppressor. Jesus was an outlier in this respect.

The unusual interpretations of the law advanced by Jesus were grounded in this unique perspective on love, that the beneficiaries of love included everyone and that love should be the foundation and end of biblical interpretation. Where love was needed to keep the law, Jesus advocated for changes of the heart. We see this in his rulings on murder and adultery. Where love required greater fidelity to commitment, he taught that we should always keep our word. We see this in his rulings on divorce and oaths. Where love conflicted with the literal teachings of Scripture, Jesus pointed us in the opposite direction. We see this in his judgments about retribution and our enemies. Certainly, though to varying degrees, these interpretations stretched the apparent limits of the law of Moses and in cases seemed to directly conflict with it.

The debate between Jesus and Jewish leaders about divorce, in Matt 19, to which we'll now turn, provides an opportunity to further explore this issue.

A Debate about Divorce
(Matt 19:1–12)

The comment of Jesus on divorce in his sermon (Matt 5:31–32) represented the tip of an iceberg in his theological debate with the rabbis about this issue. His teaching, that divorce was permitted only in cases and not always, came into direct conflict with the written law of Moses (see Deut 24:1). The issue arises again, with more detail, in Matt 19. Here the Pharisees hoped to prove that Jesus, by contradicting Moses, had broken faith with Judaism and its law. While the question they posed to him was superficially innocent, within the context of Matthew as a whole the intention was certainly malicious (Luz 2001:488–89):

> Some Pharisees came to him to test him. They asked, "Is it lawful for a man to divorce his wife for any and every reason?" (Matt 19:3)

Although Jesus did not always base his opinions on biblical texts, for he taught "as one with authority, not like the teachers of the law" (Matt 7:29), in this case he explicitly cited Scripture to support his view of divorce. This was his answer:

> "Haven't you read," he replied, "that at the beginning the Creator 'made them male and female,' and said, 'For this reason a man will leave his father and mother and be united to his wife, and the two will become one flesh'? So they are no longer two, but one flesh. Therefore what God has joined together, let no one separate." (Matt 19:3–6)

Jesus appeals in his argument to the biblical creation story, specifically to Gen 2:23–24, which describes the union of husband and wife in terms of an insoluble union. His basic logic is that the woman was originally taken from the man (Gen 2:21–22) and that marriage therefore restores this original unity. Neudecker (2014:75–76) points out that, in the days of Jesus, the rabbinic teachers apparently avoided this theme because it implied that the first Adam was androgynous rather than male only. Next to Jesus, only Philo of Alexandria talks like this in the first century (Neudecker 2014:74).

At any rate, Jesus apparently believed that the teaching of Genesis was more foundational and basic, in terms of the divine order and hence in terms of love, than the law in Deuteronomy that permitted divorce at any time. The rabbis called this interpretive strategy *qal wa-homer*, literally "light and heavy," because it placed a higher theological priority on some texts rather than others. It was one of several rules used by rabbis within the Hillel tradition to resolve apparent conflicts and contradictions in Scripture (Strack and Billerbeck 1991:18–20).

One can easily anticipate the next question from the Pharisees. Paraphrased, it would run like this: "If you are right about all of this, Jesus, then why did Moses *command* us to divorce her in the first place?" (Matt 19:7). The word choice in this question was not accidental. By casting this law as a "command" (v., *entellō*), the enemies of Jesus asserted that Moses not only permitted but actually directed them to seek a divorce when they wanted one.[11] Jesus, unflustered, responded with what was at the time a theological bombshell:

> It was because you were so hard-hearted that Moses permitted you to divorce your wives, but from the beginning it was not so. (19:7–8)[12]

Again, the word choice is intentional and significant. Jesus does not accept that Moses "commanded" divorce but rather that he "permitted" it (v., *epitrepō*) because of Israel's "hardness of heart" (*sklērokardia*). Hardly a greater spiritual insult could have been cast by Jesus, since *sklērokardia* connected thematically with Old Testament descriptions of Pharaoh's "hard heart," which caused him to enslave and persecute the Jews, and with the stubborn hearted idolater, who the Lord would "never be willing to forgive" (cf. Exod 7:23; Deut 29:18–20).

In order to draw out the full implication of this debate, we must briefly step back from the present text to consider the gospel of Matthew as a whole. As is well known among scholars, Matthew organized and shaped his gospel to present Jesus as the fulfillment of the prophecy in Deut 18:15, that God would someday send to Israel a prophet like Moses (Allison 1993; Lierman 2004; Sparks 2006). The parallels between the two biographies are striking once

11. The intention may be inferred from the fact that Matthew has reversed the language used in his Markan source. In Mark (10:2–4), Jesus speaks of a "commandment" and the Pharisees of "permission," whereas the opposite is true in Matthew (Luz 2001:490).

12. I have slightly edited the NRSV, replacing the original "allowed" with my preference, "permitted."

one realizes what's going on. Just as Pharaoh killed the Israelite children in the days of Moses, so Herod killed the Jewish children. Just as Moses was saved from Pharaoh by placing him in the Nile, so was Jesus saved from Herod by taking him to Egypt. Just as Moses departed from Egypt as the savior of Israel, so Jesus departed from Egypt as the savior of the world. Just as Moses fasted for forty days in the wilderness, so Jesus fasted for forty days. Just as Moses returned from his fast to deliver the law on Mount Sinai, so Jesus returned from his fast to deliver the Sermon on the Mount (Matt 5–7). In this sermon, Jesus said things like this: "You have heard that it was said (by Moses), but I say unto you (something else)." Further evidence for the Mosaic shape of Matthew's Jesus is found not only in the early chapters of the narrative but also in the book's overarching redactional structure, which the evangelist seems to have cast in five sections to mimic the five books of the Pentateuch. And then, at the end of Matthew's gospel, we're given one of his most profound transformations of his Mosaic Jesus: Whilst Moses commanded his people to enter the land of Canaan in order to kill "all the nations" (*panta ta ethnē*),[13] Jesus commanded his people "to make disciples of all the nations" (*panta ta ethnē*).[14] By this Matthew transformed the genocide of Deuteronomy into a Gospel conquest. Matthew accentuated the higher authority of Jesus, and the better quality of his command in this case, by portraying Jesus as speaking *on a mountain within the land* and by promising to *be with them* on their mission to the nations (Matt 28:16, 20); Moses, by contrast, spoke *on a mountain outside of the land* because he was not qualified to enter it and for this reason he admitted that he *could not go with them* (Deut 31:2).

When we understand Jesus as the new Moses of Matthew, we better understand the "theological bombshell" of his teaching in the Sermon on the Mount and on divorce in Matt 19. By teaching as "one with authority" (Matt 7:29; 9:6; 28:18), even to the extent of declaring that parts of the law permitted sin and were immoral to follow, Jesus asserted the final authority of God to say through

13. See LXX Deut 11:23; Josh 23:4; 24:18
14. Matt 28:18–20.

Scripture whatever needed to be said in light of love for God and neighbor. In some cases this called for deeper and more radical commitments to what was written in Scripture and in others for radical departures from it. As Jesus saw it, wherever the written law did not advance the cause of love, one should not assume that it was spiritually safe to follow it. Although Jesus specifically claims that this did not involve an abolishment of the law per se, it certainly involved an abolishment of certain elements in it. This is why the author of Ephesians could say that Christ made peace "by *abolishing* in his flesh the law of commandments and ordinances" (Eph 2:15, italics mine). I have always appreciated Paul Ricoeur's take on this issue, when he says that in Christ "the novelty abolishes the Scripture *and* fulfills it (Ricoeur 1980: 23).

We will next consider a debate between Jesus and his opponents about the proper observance of the Jewish Sabbath (Matt 12; Mark 2), but one further point should be made about his stance on divorce. Although Jesus exercised his authority over Scripture with greater freedom than even the "liberal" school of Hillel gave itself, his position on divorce was very restrictive and close to the conservative position adopted by the school of Shammai, which permitted divorce only in the case of infidelity (Neudecker 2014:64–71).[15] His shocked disciples declared that marriage was not worth the risk if this was indeed the plan of God (Matt 19:10). We learn from this that Jesus, in his love-based and flexible approach to Scripture, would not have been considered either liberal or conservative in his first century context. When love called for the protection of the women and children exposed to trouble by divorce, he took a strong "conservative" stance on the issues. When love called for the protection of the guilty, such as in the law of retribution, he took a strong "liberal" stance on the issues. No matter the situation, Jesus taught that love is the law, and love is the fulfillment of the law.

---

15. The position of Jesus was more conservative still if, as some scholars believe, the exception clause was added to the story in Matthew because the original teaching (see Mark 10:2–12; Luke 16:18) provided no exceptions (see Luz 2007:250; Neudecker 2014:72, 78).

A Debate about the Sabbath
(Matt 12:1–8, Mark 2:23–28)

Jesus interpreted Scripture as "one with authority," not as the scribes and teachers of the law. I have suggested that this was a critical theme in the ministry of Jesus, in that he was asserting God's authority over our interpretations and applications of Holy Scripture. The theme arises again in Matt 12, in a story worthy of our consideration.

Jesus and his disciples were strolling through a grain field on the Sabbath, and his disciples were picking and eating heads of wheat along the way.[16] The local Pharisees saw and immediately criticized Jesus on account of this, since his disciples were evidently breaking the Sabbath law as laid out in Scripture and tradition.[17] Before we discuss the response of Jesus to their charge, let us consider this situation from the perspective of his opponents.

Honestly, the Pharisees appear to have the exegetical cards on their side. Sabbath-keeping is the first ritual introduced in the Bible, was observed even by God himself, and is a prominent element in the Ten Commandments (Gen 1; Exod 20:8–11). All of this is supplemented by laws and narrative commentaries that forbade certain common activities on the Sabbath, including harvesting and gathering food (Exod 16; 34:21). Exodus 31:14–15 eventually made the actual punishment for Sabbath-breaking crystal clear: "You shall keep the Sabbath, because it is holy for you; everyone who profanes it shall be put to death." Nothing further is said in

16. For reasons that needn't concern us here, some of them understandable, many scholars believe that Jesus never contended with other Jews about the Sabbath law (Bultmann 1963:16; Sanders 1985:264–67). It is supposed instead that Christians living after Jesus responded to Jewish controversies by projecting their own situation back into the days of Jesus. While I disagree with this approach to the Sabbath controversies (see Wright 1996:390–96), in the end I don't care all that much when it comes to theology. Either Jesus himself, or later Christians reflecting back on the implications of his life and teachings, thought it important to take issue with certain ways of understanding and applying the Mosaic Sabbath laws. So we should attend closely to their observations.

17. For the oral law on Sabbath-keeping, see m. Shab. (Danby 1933: 100–121).

Exodus about the law, leaving readers with important questions. How rigorous should our observance and policing of the Sabbath laws be, and by what means shall we enforce the punishment? The answers to these questions are eventually provided in the book of Numbers, in a short but poignant story:

> When the Israelites were in the wilderness, they found a man gathering sticks on the Sabbath day. Those who found him gathering sticks brought him to Moses, Aaron, and to the whole congregation. They put him in custody, because it was not clear what should be done to him. Then the Lord said to Moses, "The man shall be put to death; all the congregation shall stone him outside the camp." The whole congregation brought him outside the camp and stoned him to death, just as the Lord had commanded Moses. (Num 15:32–36).

What shall we do when someone actually labors on the Sabbath? Stone him. This is the law's answer. The Sabbath was obviously a matter of considerable importance . . . In our parlance, it was a big (very big!) deal. Whatever we think of Jesus's exegesis, we can readily understand why the Pharisees were so troubled by what they saw. In the spirit of these and other biblical texts, it indeed seems that man was "created to keep the Sabbath."

Now Jesus did not respond, as many later Christians would, with a claim that the Sabbath had been abolished,[18] nor did he offer a new reading of the Sabbath texts themselves. He seems to have agreed that the law forbids work on the Sabbath. Still, his engagement with Sabbath law differed from that of his opponents. Said Jesus:

> Have you never read what David did when he was in need and hungry, he and those who were with him . . . How he entered the house of God when Abiathar was high priest and ate the sacred bread which it is not lawful for any but the priests to eat, and also gave it to those who were with him? . . . The Sabbath was made for man,

18. For the thoughts of Chrysostom and Cyril of Alexandria, see Simonetti 2001:234; cf. Allison 2005:160.

not man for the Sabbath. (Mark 2:25–27; adapted from
NRSV; cf. 1 Sam 21:1–6)

Either Jesus or the gospel writer was confused about the actual
high priest, who was Ahimelech not Abiathar (1 Sam 21:1), but
this is beside the point. Here Jesus cited a canonical story in which
the letter of the law was set aside for the welfare of human beings. He inferred from the text, by applying again the rule of *qal
wa-ḥomer*, that his hungry disciples were likewise exempted from
culpability. Of course we are Christians and ready to side with Jesus on this point, but if we withhold judgment for even a moment
and consider the debate in its details, there seem to be various gaps
in the argument of Jesus.

We have noted above that Sabbath observance was far more
central to biblical law and Jewish practice than the holiness of the
sacred bread, and the application of 1 Samuel to the situation of Jesus and his disciples seems a stretch. Whereas David and his men
were running unexpectedly for their lives and in need of supplies for
the trip, Jesus and his disciples knew full well that the Sabbath was
coming and, at any rate, could have fasted for a day.[19] Apart from our
Christian bias, why should we side with Jesus in this debate?

Jesus interpreted Scripture better than his critics because
his reading of the law was grounded in human empathy and af-
fection rather than in keeping the Law for its own sake. Or, as
expressed in his own words, "The Sabbath is for man, not man
for the Sabbath." Scholars have long noted that this approach to
the Sabbath did not originate with Jesus, for something like it was
known in the rabbinic traditions[20] and, at any rate, Jewish law had
established already that Sabbath rules could be set aside to save
a life (*pîqûaḥ nefeš*).[21] But the Pharisees who opposed Jesus were

19. I disagree (as does Allison) with those scholars who suggest that Jesus'
disciples were not desperately hungry, but this does not negate my basic point
(Allison 2005:162).

20. Rabbi Simeon ben Menasya (c. AD 180) said, "The Sabbath has been
committed to you and not you to the Sabbath" (see Mek. de R. Ishmael on
Exod 31:14 in Lauterbach 2004:2.494).

21. See b. Šabb. 132A; b. Yoma 83A in the Talmud.

either not of this ilk or were not prepared to go as far as Jesus was in relaxing the Law's written letter. For Jesus was not contending only for a legal exception to save human life; he was making a more far-reaching case that anything should be permitted on the Sabbath that advances the welfare of human beings. As he expressed it to the Pharisees:

> If you had known what this means, "I desire mercy and not sacrifice," you would not have condemned the guiltless. For the Son of Man is lord of the Sabbath. (Matt 12:7–8)

Jesus not only quotes Scripture to support the theological priority of love over ritual (in this case Hos 6:6) but also claims that his special authority stands behind this reading of Scripture. He claims that he is "lord of the Sabbath," in a manner reminiscent of his reputation for teaching as "one with authority." As I pointed out earlier in this discussion, Jesus, in his handling of Scripture, was asserting the authority of God over Scripture's interpretation and application to the life of his people.

In the language I've adopted for these lectures, Jesus would therefore represent Contextualism more than Foundationalism. Certainly, he took Scripture very seriously. But he saw in Scripture certain texts about love that pointed beyond Scripture to the fundamental principles necessary for its proper interpretation. These principles, which he applied with authority to the text, revealed that some biblical texts, if embraced in their natural sense of meaning, do more harm than good.

Jesus and the Temple "Cleansing" (Mark 11:15–18)

With all of this talk of love, we cannot but think about the famous incident in which Jesus angrily drove out of the Jerusalem temple those conducting business in it (Mark 11:15–19). It is widely agreed among scholars that this incident, as much as any other, triggered his eventual arrest and execution (Sanders 1985:296–308). I cannot possibly give to this incident the attention it deserves in these

lectures, but a few points should be accentuated if we're to understand the anger of Jesus in the context of his preaching about love
for God and neighbor. The relevant version of this story in Mark's
gospel is as follows:

> Then they came to Jerusalem. And he entered the temple
> and began to drive out those who were selling and those
> who were buying in the temple, and he overturned the ta-
> bles of the money changers and the seats of those who sold
> doves; and he would not allow anyone to carry anything
> through the temple. He was teaching and saying, "Is it not
> written, 'My house shall be called a house of prayer for all
> the nations'? 'But you have made it a den of robbers.'" And
> when the chief priests and the scribes heard it, they kept
> looking for a way to kill him. (Mark 11:15–18)

Jesus does not reveal directly in his words the cause of offense, but
it is obvious he found some sort of hypocrisy going on. This is evident in his quotations from two prophetic texts, one, Isa 56:7, which
proclaimed that the temple should be a sanctuary for all peoples, not
for Jews only, and another, Jer 7:11, where the prophet complained
that Israel had turned the temple into a "fake news" sanctuary for
those in active rebellion against God. Beyond this, there is much
debate about what was going on his in his mind (Luz 2005:11–12;
Evans 2012:360–63). Did his action symbolize the Temple's future
destruction? Did it symbolize a restoration of true worship? Was he
attacking the economic oppression by the establishment? Perhaps
there is some truth in all of these explanations.

Here I will point out that the sellers had set themselves up
in what was called the "Court of the Gentiles," the space set aside
to welcome non-Jews into the community of God. That the Jews
had set up shop in this space appears to have set him off, as we see
in his comment that the temple should be a house of prayer *for
all nations*. I suspect that it angered him to see that establishment
Judaism was erecting yet another wall of separation between the
human beings Jesus longed to bring together. Regardless, it is clear
that Jesus found hypocrisy and injustice in what was going on in the
temple. Love is generally patient and kind, but it can become angry

when zealous to restore broken relationships. Jesus, in the temple incident, demonstrated this about as clearly as he could.

Jesus, the Father, and the Spirit

Our discussion of the exegesis of Jesus is to an extent incomplete if we do not at least mention, on the one hand, his spiritual preparation for biblical interpretation, and, on the other, its practical result. In terms of preparation, it was apparently his habit to withdraw from his disciples and the growing crowds in order to meet his heavenly Father in prayer (Matt 14:23; 26:36–46; Mark 1:35; 6:46; Luke 5:15–16). We witness the effect of this in Mark chapter 1, where Jesus, immediately after his prayer, launches out into a new phase of his ministry: "Let us go on to the neighboring towns, so that I may proclaim the message there also; for that is what I came out to do" (Mark 1:38). We're rarely told the content of his prayers, but the exceptions provide some significant details. We see him praying before his death for the courage to follow through with his redemptive task (14:32–42), and we see him pray, in John, for his disciples in preparation for his impending death (John 13–17). Although Christian orthodoxy holds that Jesus was divine, this apparently did not mean that he carried out his work apart from an intimate relationship with and support from the Father.

Tradition holds that the Holy Spirit was also active in directing and supporting Jesus during his ministry. Early in his ministry, the Spirit descended upon him at Baptism and then led him out into the wilderness for a face-to-face bout with temptation (Matt 3:16; 4:1–11). Where Adam and Eve failed, Jesus succeeded. And after this victory, his ministry was launched.

It is much easier, in my view, to discuss the concrete elements of biblical interpretation than to explore the spiritual elements of reading Scripture. Context, language, and genre—and even interpretive strategies—can be discussed with reference to "objective" facts and conceptual ideas. But to talk about the Spirit's role in interpretation takes us into the mysterious world of prayer and meditation and fasting, where disciplines of the Spirit open us up to see the world more clearly through the eyes of God. While this avenue of interpretation is open to all and should be pursued by all, only the masters seem able to discern and explain something of this spiritual process, and even they admit to so many mysteries. What we should not do is ignore in our conversation the spiritual nature of biblical interpretation simply because it tests the limits of our language and conceptual world. Jesus invited God the Father and God the Spirit into his exegesis. So should we.

Jesus and "Sinners"

In terms of the practical results of his exegesis, Jesus definitely took some rigid and demanding theological and ethical positions. He permitted divorce only in the worst of circumstances, and he demanded that his followers manage not only their behaviors but also their interior spiritual condition. Adultery and murder are sins of the heart before they are ever sins of action. Whereas our natural inclinations are to hate our enemies, to seek revenge, and to feel disgust towards those "unclean" in behavior or physical disease, Jesus called his disciples to cultivate entirely different core responses to these emotional triggers. Those who stood against Jesus, his opponents, mainly ignored these dimensions of the religious life. They were devoted to creating and preserving the boundaries that protected their political and social power and their illusion of spiritual superiority. As a result, they did not interpret Scripture towards the end of love. Like Job's friends, and Luther, and the theologians of the old South and Nazi German, they found and devoted themselves to those biblical texts that would support their social and personal vices. We have seen how easy this maneuver can be. This is why Jesus pressed so hard for another approach to Scripture, which restored God to his rightful place on the throne of biblical interpretation and application.

At the same time, although Jesus *raised* the bar of moral and ethical expectation, he simultaneously *lowered* the bar for fellowship. Certainly he befriended the poor and the sick, and touched and healed the lame and lepers, but he was also a happy companion

READING SCRIPTURE UNDER GOD'S AUTHORITY

of the very sinners who "broke" all of his rules and teachings. He drank and partied with the riff-raff of society and sided, in two traditions, with women who had contravened his teaching about adultery and divorce (John 4:1–41; 10:1–11). He touched lepers and blessed children, declaring that one can enter heaven only with the humility of a child. He told parables in which the "sinners" are "saved" and the "saved" are "lost" (Luke 8:9–14). Jesus conveyed the deep paradox of this soteriology to his opponents in Matt 21:31: "I tell you the truth, corrupt tax collectors and prostitutes will get into the Kingdom of God before you do."

I will not pretend to wholly understand the inner logic of this theology, but one thing seems clear. Jesus believed that the religious condition of spiritually conceited people is far more dire than of those who are careless with their spiritual health. The reason for this is that spiritual arrogance, more than any other vice, damages our ability to love others, especially our enemies. It fosters within us an unhealthy reflex, by which we move very naturally from our theological and moral commitments, whatever they may be, to a strong rejection of those who do not share these commitments. Our problem with "fake news" is not only that we sometimes believe what is false; it is that we also believe, as "fake news," that it's our spiritual job to judge and reject other people. Jesus could not have been clearer about this: "Do not judge, so that you may not be judged" (Matt 7:1).

While many factors contribute to theological systems that support this kind of arrogance, one of them is biblical Foundationalism. For the reasons we have considered already, especially in lecture four, this approach to Scripture, especially in its more rigid forms, aids and abets the creation and persistence of unhealthy, "fake news" religious communities.

Conclusions:
Reading Scripture in Two Steps

I am tempted to end at this point with what we've learned from Jesus about interpreting Holy Scripture; but several dangling questions should be addressed before concluding our discussion.

First, let us consider a rather odd question that, when answered, will have important implications for a few other questions possibly raised by these lectures. The question is: Did Jesus, in his approach to Scripture, contravene Article XX of the Articles of Religion of the Episcopal Church?[22] (As I said . . . an odd question). This article, written in 1801, states that the Church should not "expound one place of Scripture, that it be repugnant to another." In other words, the Christian should not construe Scripture in a way that imagines contradictions of substance within it. I am aware that many Episcopalians no longer link themselves closely to this kind of thinking, but let us consider it nonetheless.

Jesus, it is true, seems to have done just this when he pitted one text against another in his teachings, but his method in most cases did not imply a direct conflict within Scripture. While our sample of his exegesis is fairly small, he seems to have employed most often the rabbinic rule of *qal wa-ḥomer*, which does not hold that the texts are in conflict but that, in the nature of the case, some texts carry more theological weight than others. Thus, for example, although Jesus cited Genesis against the law of divorce in Deuteronomy, he probably believed that Jewish divorces should still follow written law. Providing a letter of divorce, as the law required, was not better than staying married; but perhaps it was better than social chaos.

In a few situations, however, it is difficult to avoid an impression that Jesus has pitted one text directly against another. In the case of divorce, he could argue that the law, with its official certificate, provided a civil remedy for unspiritual Jewish behaviors. But when Jesus prescribed non-violence rather than the law's "eye for an eye" vengeance, or when he prescribed love for enemies

22. Episcopal Church 2007: 871.

in the face of biblical commands to kill them, this solution was neither available, apparently, nor used by Jesus. What would Jesus have said if his opponents had asked: "You teach that we should love our enemies. Why, then, did God command us to kill them?" We do not know. But it seems that the argument he used in the case of divorce, that the law *responded* to the broken condition of humanity, could not have been applied directly to the cases of love and non-violence. In these cases, the law presents God as demanding rather than responding to Israel's vice. If the reader follows my train of thought here, then it seems to me that there is only one option for us. Namely, that Jesus, if we could ask him our imaginary question and if he decided to answer it , , , and we must remember that he sometimes did not answer questions . . . he would have provided an answer close to what we earlier noted from C. S. Lewis and, to an extent, from Saint Augustine. Wherever Scripture appears to present God behaving badly, this cannot be an accurate portrait of God. Lewis simply admits that the human authors of Scripture sometimes put the wrong words in God's mouth, and Augustine turns to allegory.

Actually, I believe that Jesus answered this question in his own way. We have noted at several points that he taught "as one with authority" rather than as a mere teacher of the law, and that in the debate about the Sabbath he proclaimed himself the "Lord of the Sabbath." As I see it, this was his way of resolving the conflicting texts of Scripture. Because God is love and the end of Scripture is love, he showed his followers how to read Scripture when God appears to say things that God would never say.

If this be true, then the answer to our question, whether Jesus contravened Episcopal Article XX, depends on an important but subtle distinction. Respecting the human discourse of Scripture, it seems that Jesus accepted the dark influence of humanity on the written law. He attributed this to the hard heart of humanity and, presumably, to our natural limitations. But if we are speaking about Scripture as divine discourse, as the voice of God rather than diverse human voices, then on this level Jesus presented Scripture as harmonious. When properly understood, Scripture always points us to love from beginning to end. Where Scripture is good and healthy, it points us to God's redemptive remedies, most especially to his remedy in the person of Jesus Christ. Where it seems nasty, this is yet more evidence that the Bible is correct when it describes our situation as dark and dire. We, like the ancient Israelites, have our own "Canaanites" and justify our hatred by baptizing it in divine commands. Where Scripture seems to allow this, the apostle Paul was certainly correct to say: "The letter kills; but the Spirit gives life" (2 Cor 3:6).

All of this will imply, at least, that we must read Scripture in a two-step process. We must first attempt to understand what each of its human authors were saying in their respective times and places, and then we will ask what God might be saying to us through that ancient discourse. Cardinal Ratzinger (Pope Benedict) put it this way:

> Texts must first be restored to their historical locus and interpreted in their historical context. But this must be followed by a second phase of interpretation, however, in which they must also be seen in light of the entire historical movement and in terms of the central event of Christ. (Ratzinger 2008:25)

From the Protestant side Nicholas Wolterstorff provides a similar description of theological interpretation:

> We do our interpreting for divine discourse with convictions in two hands: in one hand, our convictions as to the stance and content of the appropriated discourse and the meanings of the sentences used; in the other, our convictions concerning the probabilities and improbabilities of what God would have been intending to say by appropriating this particular discourse-by-inscription. (Wolterstorff 1995:204)

Fundamental to the second task, and I suppose to the first, is that we must be wholly committed to the truth of things. For we have seen that social comfort and convenience have too often blinded the Church with "fake news," so that she's understood neither the human discourse of Scripture nor the spirit-guided voice of God. It is obvious, theologically and experientially, that this theological task will never be a fool-proof exercise. Mistakes will be made, sometimes horrible mistakes. But Jesus did recommend, or command, the best safeguard possible: that we read Scripture in a way that begins and ends with love for God and neighbor, including our enemies.

Conclusions

"Scripture aims for its readers to embark on a journey of theological formation bounded only by the character and purpose of God."

—JOEL GREEN[1]

I have described during these lectures two basic approaches to our understanding and proper reading of Scripture. Foundationalism and Contextualism, the names I've given to them, are sister approaches in certain respects. Each assumes that the Bible is both divine and human in character, and each assumes that attention should therefore be given to the natural human discourse of Scripture as well as to the the divine discourse that integrates these human perspectives into a sensible whole.

We have noted that one of the primary differences between these two views regards the extent of the Bible's humanity. The foundational view holds that God, as the ultimate author of Scripture, has "protected" the Bible from the distorting effects of the finite and fallen perspectives of its human authors. The result is a book that is essentially perfect and without any errors of substance. It is thus assumed in this approach that the meanings conveyed by the human authors are precisely the same as, though perhaps more limited than, the meanings conveyed by God.

1. Green 2007:61. I couldn't agree more. Although Green is a prominent scholar within the evangelical tradition, where biblical Foundationalism predominates, his theological sensitivities lean in a contextual direction.

Contextualists believe, to the contrary, that God did not protect the Bible as just described but instead permitted the human authors to say whatever they said as his authorized representatives. On this account of Scripture, the Church should certainly read and take seriously the testimony of these authors but should not assume that they are the unassailable spokespersons for God. The human authors of Scripture sometimes took up positions that were contrary to each other and contrary to our general knowledge about the world. This means, of course, that the meanings conveyed by Scripture's human authors are never precisely the same as whatever God is saying to his people and in some cases may actually conflict with God's voice.

I have suggested in these lectures (more than suggested, I suppose) that the available evidence strongly favors Contextualism over biblical Foundationalism. The human authors of Scripture do not offer wholly consistent views of history, theology, and moral behavior, nor can their views be squared in all cases with the modern insights of natural and social science. Just as important, and perhaps more important, is that the interpretive habits of Jesus, in his readings of Scripture, reflect assumptions that are closer to the contextual viewpoint. He actively exposed and openly confronted the tensions within Scripture. While he sometimes resolved these using the hermeneutical tools of his own culture, such as the rabbinic rule of *qal wa-ḥomer*, his Contextualism is most evident in his exercises of divine authority. Where Scripture simply conflicted with Scripture, he declared, as the God of Scripture, that love must determine which speaks for God; the other does not. Though it is seldom pointed out, that Jesus would assert love in this way means that he was counting on our natural, God-given, human capacities for love to provide dependable points of reference in biblical interpretation. While it is true that we learn about love from the Bible, it is just as true that our sense of love tells us how to read the Bible. This interdependent cycle of interpretation is an example of what scholars call the "hermeneutical circle" (Mantzavinos 2016:6–9).

Such an approach to Scripture, which focuses on love as its proper end, carries with it an implication that Scripture should point the reader not only to the message but also to God's messenger. Jesus said something like this, according to John's gospel, when he criticized his opponents with these words: "You search the scriptures because you think that in them you have eternal life; and it is they that testify on my behalf. *Yet you refuse to come to me to have life*" (John 5:39–40, italics mine). God, in Jesus, is the ultimate source of love. He is the vine; we are the branches.

The author of John was familiar with many stories about Jesus that he did not include in his gospel (John 21:25). That he has preserved this particular tradition, with its criticism of Jesus's opponents, would suggest that these words of Jesus are especially important for his actual and potential followers. What was the point? If we read the text again slowly and deliberately, I believe we'll find at least two very important implications. First, we learn that God's people, whether Jews or Christians, have often misunderstood the nature and purpose of Scripture. And second, that we do this in many cases out of spiritual blindness rather than mere ignorance. This blindness causes us to prefer "fake news" about the Bible rather than true and actual news about it and, because of this, to side with "fake news" about lots of other things. I outlined in lecture four some of the practical and spiritual results, which are not always but can be catastrophic. Humans have devised many ways to escape the authoritative role of God in our lives. Biblical Foundationalism, in many of its forms, turns out to be one of these dangerous schemes.

Each of us stands in a different place in terms of our faith, traditions, and experiences. I suspect that some readers have found in my lectures what they already believed, some are relieved to find another way forward, some are now more confused than before the lectures, and some are troubled or angered by my approach to Holy Scripture. These impressions will be related, probably, to natural assumptions about the motives of my lectures, to the effect that I have aimed to point us in particular directions on the big political, social, moral, and ethical questions of our day. While I have assumed a theological position on several retrospectively safe issues, including slavery and Nazi anti-Semitism, it is only on the issue of hitting of children that I've tackled an active debate within the orthodox Churches. With this I've provided an example, but I leave it to you, the reader, to consider the example and whether and how it applies to other issues we now face. Do I, personally, believe that it applies to these issues? Obviously, I do. In the same way that foundationalists have believed "fake news" about corporal punishment, they've believed "fake news" about lots of other things.

That said, there is plenty of "fake news" to go around. We're all human, and all of us naively and even willingly embrace deceptive and false testimonies. If we're seriously interested in kicking our "fake news" habit for an all-out commitment to the truth, we should not construe this as a transition from one side of the political and social ledger to the other. As we have seen, Jesus was very conservative on some issues and quite liberal on others. It is a serious mistake, I think, to imagine him as an ancient representative of our modern agendas. He was a man of love and justice, who demanded righteousness from his followers but extended tremendous grace when they failed. He insisted on holiness but stood against readings of Scripture that used holiness to divide humanity. Given all of this, we should not assume too quickly that we've understood the divine agenda for God's representatives in the twenty-first century. But we can know in advance that this agenda, whatever it is, will result in thoughts and deeds that demonstrate God's love for our neighbor.

I will end these lectures as I began, with these wise words from the Apostle Paul: "Consider everything but hold fast to what is good" (1 Thess 5:21).

Bibliography

Adams, Robert Nerrihew. (1999). *Finite and Infinite Goods: A Framework for Ethics*. Oxford: Oxford University.

Alcock, John. (2001). *The Triumph of Sociobiology*. Oxford: Oxford University.

Allison, Dale C. (1993). *The New Moses. A Matthean Typology*. Minneapolis: Fortress.

————. (2005). *Resurrecting Jesus: The Earliest Christian Tradition and Its Interpreters*. New York: T. & T. Clark.

Alston, William P. (1964). *Philosophy of Language*. Englewood Cliffs, NJ: Prentice-Hall.

————. (2000). *Illocutionary Acts and Sentence Meaning*. Ithaca, NY: Cornell University.

An, S., M. Marks, and D. Trafimow. (2016). "Affect, Emotion, and Cross-cultural Differences in Moral Attributions." *Current Research in Social Psychology* 24:1–12.

Anderson, Robert T. and Terry Giles. (2005). *Tradition Kept: The Literature of the Samaritans*. Peabody, MA: Hendrickson.

Aquinas, Thomas, St. (1981). *Summa Theologica*. Translated by the Fathers of the English Dominican Province. 5 vols. Notre Dame: Ave Maria.

Archer, Gleason L. (1982). *Encyclopedia of Bible Difficulties*. Grand Rapids: Zondervan.

Augustine, St. (1982). *The Literal Meaning of Genesis*. Translated by John Hammond Taylor. 2 vols. Ancient Christian Writers 41–42. New York: Paulist, 1982.

————. (1887a). "The Confessions of St. Augustine." Translated by . J. F. Shaw. In *Nicene and Post-Nicene Fathers (First Series)*, 1:29–213. 14 vols. New York: Christian Literature Co.

————. (1887b). "On Christian Doctrine." Translated by J. F. Shaw. In *Nicene and Post-Nicene Fathers (First Series)*, 2:522–97. 14 vols. New York: Christian Literature Co.

Austin, J. L. (1962). *How To Do Things with Words: The Williams James Lectures Delivered at Harvard University in 1955*. Cambridge: Harvard University Press.

Ayala, Francisco Jose. (2010). "The Theory of Evolution." In *The New Encyclopædia Britannica: Macropaedia*, 18:855–92. 32 vols. 15th ed. Chicago: Encyclopædia Britannica.

Balserak, Jon. (2002). "'The Accommodating Act Par Excellence?': An Inquiry into the Incarnation and Calvin's Understanding of Accommodation." *SJT* 55:408–23.

Balthasar, Hans Urs von. (1991). *Unless You Become Like This Child.* Translated by Erasmo Leiva-Merikakis. San Francisco: Ignatius. German orig: von Balthasar (1988). *Wenn ihr nicht werdet wie dieses Kind.* Ostfildern: Schwabenverlag.

Bartov, Omer, and Phyllis Mack, eds. (2001). *In God's Name: Genocide and Religion in the Twentieth Century.* Studies on War and Genocide 4. New York: Berghahn.

Béchard, Dean P. *The Scripture Documents: An Anthology of Official Catholic Teachings.* Collegeville, MN: Liturgical, 2002.

Beilby, James K., and Paul Rhodes Eddy. (2009). *The Historical Jesus: Five Views.* Downers Grove, IL: IVP Academic.

Benin, Stephen D. (1993). *The Footprints of God: Divine Accommodation in Jewish and Christian Thought.* Albany: State University of New York Press.

Benovitz, Moshe. (1998). *KOL NIDRE: Studies in the Development of Rabbinic Votive Institutions.* BJS 315. Atlanta: Scholars.

Beversluis, John. (2007). *C. S. Lewis and the Search for Rational Religion.* Rev. ed. Amherst, NY: Prometheus.

Bohak, Gideon. (1997). "Sadducees." In *The Oxford Dictionary of the Jewish Religion*, edited by R. J. Zwi Werblowsky and Geoffrey Wigoder, 600. Oxford: Oxford University Press, 600.

Bonhoeffer, Dietrich. (2004). *Reflections on the Bible: Human Word and Word of God.* Translated by M. Eugene Boring. Peabody, MA: Hendrickson.

Bonsirven, Joseph. (1952), "Hora Talmudica: La notation chronologique de Jean 19, 4 aurait-elle un sens symbolique?" *Bib* 33:511–15.

Boyd, Robert, and Joan B. Silk. (2009). *How Humans Evolved.* 5th ed. New York: Norton.

Brooke, John Hedley. (1991). *Science and Religion: Some Historical Perspectives.* Cambridge: Cambridge University Press.

Brown, Raymond E. (1970), *The Gospel according to John: Chapters 13–21* (AB; Garden City, NY: Doubleday).

Bultmann, Rudolf. (1963). *The History of the Synoptic Tradition.* Translated by John Marsh. New York: Harper & Row.

Calvin, John. (1845). *Commentary on the Book of* Psalms. 5 vols. Edinburgh: Calvin Translation Society.

———. (1846). *Opera Exegetica et Homiletica: Commentarius in Epistolam Pauli [et al].* Edited by C. G. Bretschneider. Corpus Reformatorum 77. Ioannis Calvini Opera Quae Supersunt Omnia 49. Braunschweig: Schwetschke.

————. (1847). *Commentaries on the First Book of Moses, called Genesis.* 2 vols. Edinburgh: Calvin Translation Society.

————. (1949). *Institutes of the Christian Religion.* Translated by Henry Beveridge. 2 vols. London: James Clarke.

Carson, D. A. (1984). "Matthew." In *Expositor's Bible Commentary.* Vol. 8, *Matthew, Mark, Luke,* edited by Frank E. Gaebelein et al. 3–599. Grand Rapids: Zondervan.

Cary, Phillip. (2019). *The Meaning of Protestant Theology: Luther, Augustine, and the Gospel that Gives Us Christ.* Grand Rapids: Baker.

Cassuto, Umberto. (1967). *A Commentary on the Book of Exodus.* Jerusalem: Magnes.

Chevalier-Skolnikoff, Suzanne. (1973). "Facial Expression of Emotion in Nonhuman Primates." In *Darwin and Facial Expression: A Century of Research in Review,* edited by Paul Ekman, 11–87. New York: Academic Press.

Chinwalla, Asif T, et al. (2002). "Initial Sequencing and Comparative Analysis of the Mouse Genome." *Nature* 420:520–62.

Clifford, Richard J. (1999). *Proverbs: A Commentary.* OTL. Louisville: Westminster John Knox.

Coggins, R. J. (1975). *Samaritans and Jews: The Origins of Samaritanism Reconsidered.* Growing Points in Theology. Atlanta: John Knox.

Collins, Adela Yarbro. (2007). *Mark: A Commentary.* Hermeneia. Minneapolis: Fortress.

Crenshaw, James L. (1980). *Old Testament Wisdom.* Atlanta: John Knox.

Danby, Herbert. (1933). *The Mishnah.* Oxford: Oxford University.

Darwin, Charles. (1897). *Expression of the Emotions in Man and Animals.* New York: Applegate.

De Santillana, Giorgio. (1955). *The Crime of Galileo.* Chicago: University of Chicago Press.

Dexinger, Ferdinand. (1989). "Samaritan Eschatology." In *The Samaritans,* edited by Alan D. Crown, 266–92. Tübingen: Mohr/Siebeck.

Ekman, Paul, ed. (1973). *Darwin and Facial Expression: A Century of Research in Review.* New York: Academic Press.

Ekman, Paul, and Wallace V. Friesen. (1975). *Unmasking the Face: A Guide to Recognizing Emotions from Facial Expressions.* Englewood Cliffs, NJ: Prentice-Hall.

Elliott, E. N., ed. (1860). *Cotton Is King, and Pro-Slavery Arguments: Comprising the Writings of Hammond, Harper, Christy, Stringfellow, Hodge, Bledsoe, and Cartwright.* Augusta, GA: Pritchard, Abbott & Loomis.

Episcopal Church. (2007). *The Book of Common Prayer.* New York: Church Publishing.

Espeland, Rune Hjalmar. (2007). *When Neighbours Become Killers: Ethnic Conflict and Communal Violence in Western Uganda.* Bergen: Chr. Michelsen Institute.

Evans, Craig A. (2005). *Ancient Texts for New Testament Studies: A Guide to the Background Literature.* Peabody, MA: Hendrickson.

———. (2012). *Matthew.* NCamBC. Cambridge: Cambridge University Press.

Finnis, John. (2011). *Natural Law and Natural Rights.* 2nd ed. Oxford: Oxford University Press.

Fitzmyer, Joseph A. (1981–1984). *The Gospel according to Luke.* 2 vols. AB 28, 28A. Garden City, NY: Doubleday.

———. (1998). *The Acts of the Apostles.* AB 31. New York: Doubleday.

Fowler, Harold North, ed. (1942). "The Apology." In *Euthyphro, Apology, Crito, Pheodo, Phaedrus,* 69–145. LCL. Cambridge: Harvard University Press.

Fox, Michael V. (2009). *Proverbs 10–31.* Anchor Yale Bible 18B. New Haven: Yale University Press.

Gershoff, Elizabeth T., and Andrew Grogan-Kaylor. (2016). "Spanking and Child Outcomes: Old Controversies and New Meta-Analyses." *Journal of Family Psychology* 30:453–69.

Gingerich, Owen, and James MacLachlan. (2005). *Nicolaus Copernicus: Making the Earth a Planet.* New York: Oxford University Press.

Goldstein, David S. (2010). "Adrenal Responses to Stress." *Cellular and Molecular Neurobiology* 30:1433–40.

Gottman, John M., and Sybil Carrère. (1999). "Predicting Divorce among Newlyweds from the First Three Minutes of a Marital Conflict Discussion." *Family Process* 38:293–301.

Granitz, Neil A. and James C. Ward. (2001). "Actual and Perceived Sharing of Ethical Reasoning and Moral Intent among In-Group and Out-Group Members." *Journal of Business Ethics* 33:299–322.

Green, Joel B. (2007). *Seized by Truth: Reading the Bible as Scripture.* Nashville: Abingdon.

Green, Joel B., and Stuart L. Palmer, eds. (2005). *In Search of the Soul: Four Views of the Mind-Body Problem.* Downers Grove, IL: InterVarsity.

Greenberger, Ben Tzion. (1997). "Inspiration." In *The Oxford Dictionary of the Jewish Religion,* edited by R. J. Zwi Werblowsky and Geoffey Wigoder, 352–53. Oxford: Oxford University Press.

Greene-McCreight, K. E. (1999). *Ad Litteram: How Augustine, Calvin, and Barth Read the "Plain Sense" of Genesis 1–3.* Issues in Systematic Theology 5. Frankfurt: Lang.

Gregory the Great. (2004). "Moralia in Job." In *History of Biblical Interpretation: A Reader,* edited by William Yarchin, 88–92. Peabody, MA: Hendrickson.

Greven, Philip. (1990). *Spare the Child: The Religious Roots of Punishment and the Psychological Impact of Physical Abuse.* New York: Vintage.

Gritsch, Eric W. (2012). *Martin Luther's Anti-Semitism: Against His Better Judgment.* Grand Rapids: Eerdmans.

Gundry, Robert H. (1982). *Matthew: A Commentary on His Literary and Theological Art.* Grand Rapids: Eerdmans.

Hagen, John G. (1908). "Copernicus, Nicolaus." In *The Catholic Encyclopedia,* edited by C. G. Herbermann et al., 4:352–54. 15 vols. New York: Appleton.

Haidt, Jonathan. (2001). "The Emotional Dog and Its Rational Tail: A Social Intuitionist Approach to Moral Judgment." *Psychological Review* 108:814–34.

———. (2012). *The Righteous Mind: Why Good People Are Divided by Politics and Religion.* New York: Pantheon.

Hall, Christopher A. (1998). *Reading Scripture with the Church Fathers.* Downers Grove, IL: InterVarsity.

———. (2002). *Learning Theology with the Church Fathers.* Downers Grove, IL: InterVarsity.

Haney, C., W. Banks, and P. Zimbardo. (1973). "Interpersonal Dynamics in a Simulated Prison." *International Journal of Criminology and Penology* 1:69–97.

Haynes, Stephen R. (2002). *Noah's Curse: The Biblical Justification of American Slavery.* Oxford: Oxford University Press.

Heschel, Susannah. (2008). *The Aryan Jesus: Christian Theologians and the Bible in Nazi Germany.* Princeton: Princeton University Press.

James, William. (1902). *The Varieties of Religious Experience: A Study in Human Nature.* New York: Longmans, Green.

Jern, P., G. O. Sperber, and J. Blomberg. (2005). "Use of Endogenous Retroviral Sequences (ERVs) and Structural Markers for Retroviral Phylogenetic Inference and Taxonomy." *Retrovirology* 2, 50: doi:10.1186/1742-4690-2-50.

Johnson, Luke Timothy, and William S. Kurz. (2002). *The Future of Catholic Biblical Scholarship: A Constructive Conversation.* Grand Rapids: Eerdmans.

Johnson, Welkin E., and J. M. Coffin. (1999). "Constructing Primate Phylogenies from Ancient Retrovirus Sequences USA." *Proceedings of the National Academy of Sciences* 96:10254–60.

Kuhn, Thomas S. (1957). *The Copernican Revolution: Planetary Astronomy in the Development of Western Thought.* Cambridge: Harvard University Press.

———. (1970). *The Structure of Scientific Revolutions.* 2nd ed. Chicago: University of Chicago.

Langford, J. J. (2003). "Galilei, Galileo." In *The New Catholic Encyclopedia*, edited by Berard L. Marthaler, ed., 6:58–64. 15 vols. Detroit: Thomson Gale.

Lauterbach, J. Z. (2004). *Mekhilta de Rabbi Ishmael: A Critical Edition on the Basis of the MSS and Early Editions with an English Translation, Introduction and Notes.* 2 vols. 2nd ed. Philadelphia: Jewish Publication Society.

Lewis, C. S. (1958). *Reflections on the Psalms.* New York: Harcourt, Brace & World.

———. (2001). *The Abolition of Man.* San Francisco: HarperCollins.

Lierman, John. *The New Testament Moses: Christian Perceptions of Moses and Israel in the Setting of Jewish Religion*. WUNT 2/173. Tübingen: Mohr/ Siebeck, 2004.

Lippa, Richard A. (2005). *Gender, Nature, and Nurture*. 2nd ed. Mahwah, NJ: Erlbaum.

Livingstone, E. A., ed. (1997) "Commandments, the Ten." In *The Oxford Dictionary of the Christian Church*, edited by E. A. Livingstone, 382–83. 3rd ed. Oxford: Oxford University Press.

Long, V. Philips. (1994). *The Art of Biblical History*. Foundations of Contemporary Interpretation 5. Grand Rapids: Zondervan.

Longman, Tremper, III. (1985). "Form Criticism, Recent Developments in Genre Theory, and the Evangelical." *WTJ* 1985:46–67.

Luther, Martin. (1880–1910). *Sämtliche Schriften*. Edited by Johann Georg Walch. 23 vols. in 25. St. Louis: Concordia.

———. (1892). *Commentary on the Sermon on the Mount*. Translated by Charles A. Hay. Philadelphia: Lutheran Publication Society.

———. (1971). "On the Jews and Their Lies." In *Luther's Works*, edited by Jaroslav Pelikan et al., 47:137–306. 55 vols. Philadelphia: Fortress. German orig.: Luther. (1543). *Von den Juden und ihren Lügen*. Wittenburg: Lufft.

Luz, Ulrich. (2001). *Matthew 8–20: A Commentary*. Translated by James E. Crouch. Hermeneia. Minneapolis: Fortress.

———. (2005). *Matthew 21–28: A Commentary*. Translated by James E. Crouch. Hermeneia. Minneapolis: Fortress.

———. (2007). *Matthew 1–7: A Commentary*. Translated by James E. Crouch. Hermeneia. Minneapolis: Fortress.

Machamer, Peter K., ed. (1998). *The Cambridge Companion to Galileo*. Cambridge Companions to Philosophy. Cambridge: Cambridge University Press.

Mantzavinos, C. (2016). "Hermeneutics." In *Stanford Encyclopedia of Philosophy*, edited by Edward N. Zalta et al., 1–31. Stanford, CA: Stanford University Press.

Marshall, I. Howard. (1999). *A Critical and Exegetical Commentary on the Pastoral Epistles*. International Critical Commentary. Edinburgh: T. & T. Clark.

Marshall, Michael J. (2002). *Why Spanking Doesn't Work*. Springville, UT: Bonneville.

McKane, William. (1970). *Proverbs: A New Approach*. OTL. Philadelphia: Westminster.

Melanchthon, Philip (1846). *Opera Quae Supersunt Omnia*. Edited by C. G. Bretschneider. Corpus Reformatorum 13. Halle: Schwetschke.

Michael, Robert. (2006). *Holy Hatred: Christianity, Antisemitism, and the Holocaust*. New York: Palgrave Macmillan.

Moncrieff, Michael A., and Pierre Lienard. (2018). "Moral Judgments of In-Group and Out-Group Harm in Post-conflict Urban and Rural Croatian Communities." *Frontiers in Psychology* 23: https://doi.org/10.3389/fpsyg. 2018.00212.

Montgomery, J. A. (1907). *The Samaritans: The Earliest Jewish Sect.* Philadelphia: Winston.

Murphy, Roland E. (1990). *The Tree of Life: An Exploration of Biblical Wisdom Literature.* 3rd ed. Grand Rapids: Eerdmans.

Neudecker, Reinhard. (2014). *Moses Interpreted by the Pharisees and Jesus: Matthew's Antitheses in the Light of Early Rabbinic Literature.* Subsidia Biblica 44. Rome: Pontifical Biblical Institute Press).

Neusner, Jacob. (2000). *The Babylonian Talmud: A Translation and Commentary.* 22 vols. Peabody, MA: Hendrickson.

Newsome, James D. (1986). *A Synoptic Harmony of Samuel, Kings, and Chronicles.* Grand Rapids: Baker.

Nietzsche, Friedrich Wilhelm. (2007). *On the Genealogy of Morality.* Cambridge: Cambridge University Press. German orig: Nietzsche. (1887). *Zur Genealogie der Moral: Eine Streitschrift.* Leipzig: Naumann.

Nolan, Cathal J. (2006). *The Age of Religious Wars, 1000–1650: An Encyclopedia of Global Warfare and Civilization.* 2 vols. Westport, CT: Greenwood.

Noll, Mark A. (1994). *The Scandal of the Evangelical Mind.* Grand Rapids: Eerdmans.

————. (2011). *Jesus Christ and the Life of the Mind.* Grand Rapids: Eerdmans.

Numbers, Ronald L. (2006). *The Creationists: From Scientific Creationism to Intelligent Design.* Expanded ed. Cambridge: Harvard University Press.

O'Dowd, Ryan P. (2007). "A Chord of Three Strands: Epistemology in Job, Proverbs and Ecclesiastes." In *The Bible and Epistemology: Biblical Soundings on the Knowledge of God,* edited by Mary Healy and Robin Parry, 65–87. Milton Keynes, UK: Paternoster.

Origen. (2009). *Homilies on Numbers.* Translated by Th. P. Scheck. Downers Grove, IL: InterVarsity.

Papias of Hieropolis. (2003). "Fragments of Papias and Qadratus." In *The Apostolic Fathers,* edited by Bart D. Ehrman, 2:93–119. 2 vols. LCL 24, 25. Cambridge: Harvard University Press.

Parr, Lisa A., Bridget M. Waller, and Matthew Heintz. (2008). "Facial Expression Categorization by Chimpanzees Using Standardized Stimuli." *Emotion* 8:216–31.

Philo of Alexandria. (1929–1953). *Philo.* Edited by F. H. Colson and G. H. Whitaker. 10 vols. with 2 supplements. LCL. Cambridge: Harvard University Press.

Plutchik, Robert. (2000). *Emotions in the Practice of Psychotherapy: Clinical Implications of Affect Theories.* Washington, DC: American Psychological Association.

Plutchik, Robert, and Henry Kellerman, eds. (1980). *Emotion: Theory, Research, and Experience.* Vol. 1: *Theories of Emotion.* New York: Academic Press.

Polkinghorne, John. (2009). *Theology in the Context of Science.* New Haven: Yale University Press.

Pontifical Biblical Commission. (2014). *The Inspiration and Truth of Sacred Scripture.* Translated by T. Esposito and S. Gregg. Collegeville, MN: Liturgical.

Preus, J. Samuel. (2001). *Spinoza and the Irrelevance of Biblical Authority.* Cambridge: Cambridge University Press.

Preuschoft, Signe. (2000). "Primate Faces and Facial Expressions." *Social Research* 67:245–71.

Probst, Christopher J. (2012). *Demonizing the Jews: Luther and the Protestant Church in Nazi Germany.* Bloomington: Indiana University Press.

Rad, Gerhard von. (1972). *Wisdom in Israel.* Translated by James D. Martin. London: SCM. German orig: von Rad. (1970). *Weisheit in Israel.* Neukirchen-Vluyn: Neukirchener.

Ratzinger, Cardinal Joseph. (2008). "Biblical Interpretation in Conflict: On the Foundations and the Itinerary of Exegesis Today." In *Opening Up the Scriptures: Joseph Ratzinger and the Foundations of Biblical Interpretation,* edited by José Granados, et al., 1–29. Grand Rapids: Eerdmans, 2008.

Richardson, H. Neil. (1955). "Some Notes on לִיץ and Its Derivatives." *VT* 5:163–79.

Ricoeur, Paul. (1980). *Essays on Biblical Interpretation.* Philadelphia: Fortress.

Roberts, Robert C., and W. Jay Wood. (2007). *Intellectual Virtues: An Essay in Regulative Epistemology.* Oxford: Clarendon.

Roloff, Jürgen. (2000). *Jesus.* Beck'sche Reihe. Wissen 2142. Munich: Beck.

Rowley, H. H. (1980). *Job.* NCBC. Grand Rapids: Eerdmans.

Sanders, E. P. (1985). *Jesus and Judaism.* Philadelphia: Fortress.

Schwartz, B. (1989). *Psychology of Learning and Behavior.* 2nd ed. New York: Norton.

Schwartz, Baruch J. (1997). "Ten Commandments." In *The Oxford Dictionary of the Jewish Religion,* edited by R. J. Zwi Werblowsky and Geoffrey Wigoder, 683–84. Oxford: Oxford University Press.

Searle, J. (1969). *Speech Acts: An Essay in the Philosophy of Language.* Cambridge: Cambridge University Press.

Simonetti, Manlio. (2001). *Matthew 1–13.* ACCS. Downers Grove, IL: InterVarsity.

Smith, Tom W., Michael Hout, and Peter Marsden. (2013). *General Social Surveys, 1972–2012.* Ann Arbor, MI: Inter-university Consortium for Political and Social Research.

Snaith, Norman H. (1968). *The Book of Job: Its Origin and Purpose.* SBT 1/11. London: SCM.

Sonne, Isaiah. (1945). "The Schools of Shammai and Hillel Seen from Within." In *Louis Ginzberg: Jubilee Volume on the Occasion of His Seventieth Birthday,* 291–95. New York: American Academy for Jewish Research.

Sparks, Kenton L. (2005). *Ancient Texts for the Study of the Hebrew Bible.* Peabody, MA: Hendrickson.

———. (2006). "Gospel as Conquest: Mosaic Typology in Matthew 28, 16–20." *CBQ* 68:651–53.

————. (2008). *God's Word in Human Words: An Evangelical Appropriation of Critical Biblical Scholarship*. Grand Rapids: Baker Academic.

————. (2012). *Sacred Word, Broken Word: Biblical Authority and the Dark Side of Scripture*. Grand Rapids: Eerdmans.

Spicq, Celas. (1994). *Theological Lexicon of the New Testament*. Translated by James D. Ernest. 3 vols.. Peabody, MA: Hendrickson. French orig: Spicq. (1978–1982). *Notes de lexicographie néo-testamentaire*. 3 vols. Orbis Biblicus et Orientalis 22.1–3. Göttingen: Vandenhoeck & Ruprecht.

Spinoza, Baruch. (1640). *Tractatus theologica-politicus*. Hamburg: Künraht. English trans: Spinoza. (1989). *Tractatus theologica-politicus*. Translated by S. Shirley. New York: Brill.

Stauffer, Richard. (1971). "Calvin et Copernic." *RHR* 179:31–40.

Steigmann-Gall, Richard. (2003). *The Holy Reich: Nazi Conceptions of Christianity, 1919–1945*. Cambridge: Cambridge University Press.

Steinmetz, David C. (1980). "The Superiority of Pre-Critical Exegesis." *ThTo* 37:27–38,

Stimson, Dorothy. (1917). *The Gradual Acceptance of the Copernican Theory of the Universe*. Reprint, Gloucester, MA: Peter Smith, 1972.

Strack, Hermann L., and Günter Stemberger. (1992). *Introduction to the Talmud and Midrash*. Translated by Markus Bockmuehl. Minneapolis: Fortress.

Straus, Murray A. (2001). *Beating the Devil Out of Them: Corporal Punishment in American Families and Its Effects on Children*. New Brunswick, NJ: Transaction.

Swanson, Reuben J. (1984). *The Horizontal Line: Synopsis of the Gospels*. Pasadena, CA: William Carey Library.

Tamarin, Georges R. (1973). *The Israeli Dilemma: Essays on a Warfare State*. Publications of the Polemological Centre of the Free University of Brussels 2. Rotterdam: Rotterdam University Press.

Telushkin, Joseph. (2010). *Hillel: If Not Now, When?* New York: Schocken.

Theophylact of Ochrid. (1992). *The Explanation by Blessed Theophylact of the Holy Gospel according to St. Matthew*. House Springs, MO: Chrysostom.

Ulrich, R. E. et al. (1966). "Reflexive Fighting in Response to Aversive Stimulation." *Behavior* 26:124–29.

Vanhoozer, Kevin J. (1998). *Is There a Meaning in This Text? The Bible, the Reader, and the Morality of Literary Knowledge*. Grand Rapids: Zondervan.

Walton, John H. (2013). "A Historical Adam: Archetypal Creation View." In *Four Views on the Historical Adam*, edited by Matthew Barrett and Ardel B. Caneday, 89–118. Counterpoints: Bible & Theology. Grand Rapids: Zondervan.

Walton, John H., and D. Brent Sandy. (2013). *The Lost World of Scripture: Ancient Literary Culture and Biblical Authority*. Grand Rapids: InterVarsity.

Ware, Timothy. (1997). *The Orthodox Way*. New ed. London: Penguin.

Webb, William J. (2011). *Corporal Punishment in the Bible: A Redemptive-Movement Hermeneutic for Troubling Texts*. Downers Grove, IL: InterVarsity).

Webster, John. (2003). *Holy Scripture: A Dogmatic Sketch.* Cambridge: Cambridge University Press.

———. (2005). "Scripture, Authority of." In *Dictionary for Theological Interpretation of the Bible* , edited by Kevin J. Vanhoozer, 724–27. Grand Rapids: Baker.

Weikart, Richard. (2013). "The Role of Darwinism in Nazi Racial Thought." *German Studies Review* 36:537–56.

Welwood, John. (1984). "Principles of Inner Work: Psychological and Spiritual." *Journal of Transpersonal Psychology* 16:63–73.

Wenger, Paul D. (2005). "Discipline in the Book of Proverbs: 'To Spank or Not to Spank.'" *JETS* 48:715–32.

Wesley, John. (1872). *The Works of John Wesley.* 12 vols. London: Wesleyan Methodist Book Room.

White, Andrew Dickson. (1896). *A History of the Warfare of Science with Theology.* 2 vols. New York: Appleton.

White, Robert. (1980). "Calvin and Copernicus: The Problem Reconsidered." *CTJ* 15:233–43.

Whybray, R. N. (1994) *Proverbs.* NCBC. Grand Rapids: Eerdmans, 1994.

Wilson, E. O. (1975). *Sociobiology: A New Synthesis.* Cambridge, MA: Belknap.

———. (1978). *On Human Nature.* Cambridge: Harvard University Press.

Wolterstorff, Nicholas. (1995). *Divine Discourse: Philosophical Reflections on the Claim That God Speaks.* Cambridge: Cambridge University Press, 1995.

Wood, W. Jay. (1998). *Epistemology: Becoming Intellectually Virtuous.* Downers Grove, IL: InterVarsity.

Wrangham, Richard. (2019). *The Goodness Paradox: The Strange Relationship between Virtue and Violence in Human Evolution* (New York: Pantheon).

Wright, David F. (1986). "Calvin's Pentateuchal Criticism: Equity, Hardness of Heart, and Divine Accommodation in the Mosaic Harmony Commentary." *CTJ* 21:33–50.

Wright, N. T. (1996). *Jesus and the Victory of God.* Christian Origins and the Question of God 2. Minneapolis: Fortress.

Wuthnow, Robert. (1991). *Acts of Compassion: Caring for Others and Healing Ourselves.* Princeton: Princeton University Press.

Made in the USA
Monee, IL
24 February 2023

28602582R00080